Knowlton School of Architecture
The Ohio State University

TODD GANNON, SERIES EDITOR

ZAHA HADID
BMW CENTRAL BUILDING

SOURCE BOOKS
IN ARCHITECTURE

7

Leipzig, Germany

Todd Gannon, Volume Editor

M000036032

PRINCETON ARCHITECTURAL PRESS, NEW YORK

OTHER SOURCE BOOKS IN ARCHITECTURE:

MORPHOSIS/Diamond Ranch High School

The Light Construction Reader

BERNARD TSCHUMI/Zénith de Rouen

UN STUDIO/Erasmus Bridge

STEVEN HOLL/Simmons Hall

MACK SCOGIN MERRILL ELAM/Knowlton Hall

Published by

Princeton Architectural Press

37 East Seventh Street

New York, New York 10003

For a free catalog of books, call 1.800.722.6657.

Visit our web site at www.papress.com.

© 2006 Princeton Architectural Press

All rights reserved

Printed and bound in China

09 08 07 06 4 3 2 1 First edition

No part of this book may be used or reproduced in any manner
without written permission from the publisher, except in the
context of reviews.

Every reasonable attempt has been made to identify owners of
copyright. Errors or omissions will be corrected in subsequent
editions.

Editing: Linda Lee

Design: Jan Haux

Special thanks to: Nettie Aljian, Dorothy Ball, Nicola Bednarek,
Janet Behning, Becca Casbon, Penny (Yuen Pik) Chu, Russell
Fernandez, Pete Fitzpatrick, Clare Jacobson, John King, Mark
Lamster, Nancy Eklund Later, Katharine Myers, Lauren Nelson,
Scott Tennent, Jennifer Thompson, Paul Wagner, Joseph Weston,
and Deb Wood of Princeton Architectural Press —Kevin C. Lippert,
publisher

Library of Congress Cataloging-in-Publication Data

Hadid, Zaha.

Zaha Hadid : BMW Central Building / Todd Gannon, volume editor.

p. cm. — (Source books in architecture ; 7)

Includes bibliographical references.

ISBN-10: 1-56898-536-3

ISBN-13: 978-1-56898-536-7 (alk. paper)

1. Bayerische Motoren Werke. 2. Hadid, Zaha. 3. Architecture,
Industrial—Germany—Leipzig. 4. Leipzig (Germany)—Buildings,
structures, etc. I. Title: BMW Central Building. II. Gannon, Todd.
III. Title. IV. Series.

NA6474.B39H33 2006

725'.4—dc22

2006000035

CONTENTS

In Print
@ 29 95

ACKNOWLEDGMENTS

The tireless work of Zaha Hadid Architects has made this book possible. In particular, I thank Zaha Hadid, Patrik Schumacher, Lars Teichmann, Jim Heverin, and Lucien Smith for their effort and patience.

Robert Livesey, former director of the Knowlton School of Architecture, remains a key member of the Source Books in Architecture team. His tenacity and support keep us functioning. Friends and colleagues in Columbus, Los Angeles, New York, and elsewhere, including George Acock, Mitch Acock, Ewan Branda, Mike Cadwell, Dana Cuff, Dave DiMaria, Francesca Falchi, Diane Favro, Masha Fedorchenko, Bruce Ferguson, Kim Gannon, Tracy Gannon, Jackie Gargus, Tyler Goss, Carolyn Hank, N. Katherine Hayles, Sharon Johnston, Tali Krakowsky, Sylvia Lavin, Gustavo LeClerc, Mark Lee, José Oubrerie, Mike Meehan, Jane Murphy, Ted Musielewicz, Rick Norton, Ryan Palider, Linda Pollari, Andrew Rosenthal, Craig Robins, Vi Schaaf, Ashley Schafer, Chris Shrodes, Bob Somol, Michael Speaks, Jennifer Volland, Tim Welsh, Amit Wolf, and Jon Yoder, have made essential contributions. I would also like to thank Idoia Aristegui, Olatz Cacho, and Irene Ron, whose hospitality makes visiting London a pleasure.

Teresa Ball, Mike Denison, Laurie Gunzelman, and Luke Kautz at the Knowlton School, and Linda Lee, Jan Haux, and Kevin Lippert at Princeton Architectural Press guided the book through production and design. Finally, special thanks to Jeff Kipnis and Nicole Hill, who have been crucial to Source Books in Architecture from its inception.

SOURCE BOOKS IN ARCHITECTURE

Following the example of music publication, Source Books in Architecture offers an alternative to the traditional architectural monograph. If one is interested in hearing music, he or she simply purchases the desired recording. If, however, one wishes to study a particular piece in greater depth, it is possible to purchase the score—the written code that more clearly elucidates the structure, organization, and creative process that brings the work into being. This series is offered in the same spirit. Each Source Book focuses on a single work by a particular architect or on a special topic in contemporary architecture. The work is documented with sketches, models, renderings, working drawings, and photographs at a level of detail that allows complete and careful study of the project from its conception to the completion of design and construction.

The graphic component is accompanied by commentary from the architect and critics that further explores both the technical and cultural content of the work in question.

Source Books in Architecture was conceived by Jeffrey Kipnis and Robert Livesey and is the product of the Herbert Baumer seminars, a series of interactions between students and seminal practitioners at the Knowlton School of Architecture at The Ohio State University. After a significant amount of research on distinguished architects, students lead a discussion that encourages those architects to reveal their architectural motivations and techniques. The students record and transcribe these meetings, which become the basis for these Source Books.

The seminars are made possible by a generous bequest from Herbert Herndon Baumer. Educated at the Ecole des Beaux-Arts, Baumer was a professor in the Department of Architecture at The Ohio State University from 1922 to 1956. He had a dual career as a distinguished design professor who inspired many students and a noted architect who designed several buildings at The Ohio State University and other Ohio colleges.

November 2001
Competition Phase 1

2002/2003
Construction documents completed
Bidding and negotiations

January 2002
Competition Phase 2

March 2002
Jury decision

August 2002
Design development completed

March 2003
Construction commenced

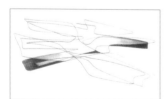

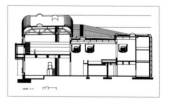

DATA AND CHRONOLOGY

BMW CENTRAL BUILDING
Leipzig, Germany

Client:
BMW AG. Munich, Germany

Site:
250,000-square-foot (23,000-square-meter) site area bounded on three sides by existing manufacturing sheds. Total Leipzig campus area: 540 acres

Area:
270,000 square feet

Program:
Control functions, offices/admin., meeting rooms, cafeteria, and public relations facilities for the BMW 3 Series manufacturing plant.

Employees in Leipzig:
5,500

Parking:
4,100 spaces

Cost:
approx. $60 million, €50 million

Data:
Load-bearing walls, floors, office cascades: Cast-in-place concrete

Roof structure: Structural steel beams and space frame

Cladding: Corrugated metal, channel glass, glass curtain walls

September 2004
Central Building completed

May 2005
Landscaping completed
Central Building opened

March 2004
Building enclosed

June 2004
Car park completed

January 2004
Structural steel completed

ARCHITECT'S STATEMENT

When BMW decided to locate their new Central Plant just outside Leipzig, one of the more prosperous cities in former East Germany, it required an unusual approach to fill the central gap between their previously designed standard factory buildings. The layout of the original plant and the positioning of the production facilities—a direct consequence of fabrication requirements—resulted in a narrow stretch of open land. This area, 295' x 950' (89 x 290 m), framed on three sides by the existing structures, was the site for the new Central Building.

The Central Building needed to respond to various, often contradictory, functional requirements, providing the technical communication between the different stages of production as well as enhance the verbal communication between the employees. BMW's aim was to stage a more transparent production process along flexible office areas within a communication network. To get as many variations on this brief as possible, BMW invited twenty-six offices of various backgrounds to compete in a staged design competition. At the end of this two-stage process, Zaha Hadid Architects emerged as the winner.

The winning design for the Central Building was as remarkable as it was unique: the ideal translation of BMW's vision of a "communication hub" into architecture. Offering spaces beyond the well known but unpopular open-office landscape of the 1970s Anglo-American corporate culture, the project is a radically new interpretation of office design. Where views were formerly blocked by room dividers and partitions, with office desks floating randomly on air-conditioned floor plates, the Central Building, with its cascades and platforms, provides maximum transparency and a high degree of spatial identification within one naturally ventilated, well-lit volume.

The Central Building acts as the nerve center of the whole factory complex. Conceived as a knot that draws together the various flows of the factory process, the Central Building connects the three main manufacturing departments, Body-in-White, Paint Shop, and Assembly, while serving as the entrance to the plant. Administrative functions, organized along a series of connective paths that erode the more enclosed technical functions on the ground floor, create an ideal opportunity to shape flows and movement into form and usable space.

Such a planning strategy does not only apply to the cycles and trajectories of workers and visitors but also to the production line, which traverses this central point. Open to view throughout the facility, cars in various stages of completion pass along their tracks between the various surrounding production units. Up to 650 cars each day silently glide through the office space on four separate lines. Every 3 series car that leaves the plant passes the Central Building four times before being delivered to its owner.

The main area of the Central Building was conceived as a "market place" intended to enhance staff communication by providing them with an area in which to avail themselves of personal and administrative services. This sequencing of the building exploits the obvious sequence of front-to-back for the distribution of public-to-private activities.

The primary organizational strategy for the office areas is the scissor-section that connects the ground floor and first floor in a continuous field. Two sequences of terraced plates, like giant staircases, step up from north to south and from south to north capturing a long connective void between them. The cascading floor plates, as large as 62' x 75' (19 x 23 m) in size, are large enough to allow for flexible occupation patterns. The advantage here lies in the articulation of recognizable domains within the overall field, while simultaneously achieving a greater degree of visual communication than would be possible with a single, flat floor plate.

The integration of blue-collar and white-collar workers is facilitated by an overall transparency of the internal organization. There is a commingling of typically disconnected functions and spaces that avoids the traditional segregation of status groups. A series of engineering and administrative functions are located within the trajectory of the manual work-force's daily movements. White-collar functions are located both on the ground level and on the first floor. Likewise, blue-collar social spaces are located on both floors, preventing the establishment of exclusive domain—the plant's restaurant, for example, is located right in the middle of the office floors attracting all workers amidst the administrative areas.

The radical rethinking of established paradigms that generated the interior solution was brought to bear on the exterior components as well. The intrinsic problems of a large parking lot in front of a building were avoided by turning it into a dynamic spectacle in its own right. The inherent dynamism of vehicle movement and a vast field of car bodies are revealed in the arrangement of parking lots, which allow the whole field to move, color, and sparkle with swooping trajectories that culminate within the building. The cars sweep underneath the bridgelike entry canopy, setting visitors down onto the glazed public lobby that allows views deep into the building.

Many visitors are expected, and BMW exposes the heart of the plant to the public by avoiding any factory gates or fencing. The Central Building was designed to be predominantly functional, but it complies equally with representational requirements, presenting the brand in an almost cinematic way.

Lars Teichmann, Project Architect,
Zaha Hadid Architects,
December 2005

ZH: Zaha Hadid, Principal, Zaha Hadid Architects
PS: Patrik Schumacher, Principal, Zaha Hadid Architects
LT: Lars Teichmann, Project Architect, Zaha Hadid Architects
TG: Todd Gannon, Series Editor, Source Books in Architecture

CONVERSATIONS WITH ZAHA HADID

Compiled and edited by Todd Gannon

TODD GANNON: **Bruce [Ferguson, Dean of the School of Arts at Columbia University] was very complimentary during our visit to the BMW Central Building yesterday. He told me it was the first time he had experienced a twenty-first-century space.**

ZAHA HADID: Yes, he told me as well. It is, of course, a very flattering comment.

I think it springs from the idea that everything moves through the building. The blue-collar and white-collar workers, the public, and, of course, the cars themselves all move through the same space. But actually, with its fascination with the car, with ideas of movement and velocity, BMW really began as a twentieth-century project.

TG: **Yes, but I would argue that your development of those ideas differs fundamentally from the factory aesthetic of the twentieth century.**

Think of the Fiat Factory in Turin or Albert Kahn's projects for Ford Motors in Detroit—projects that are very much a part of the modernist ethos of the assembly line. While at BMW you explore both the high functionalism of Ford and the expressionism of Fiat, you take a different approach.

LARS TEICHMANN: You are right; it is a different approach. Although BMW is doing serial production akin to the earlier projects you mention, it is serial production of a very different kind. If one takes into account all possible options, the BMW 3 series made here can be assembled in 10×10^{17} different configurations. This is not the serialized production of the twentieth century. It is a totally different way of producing, one hundred years from the Fordist ideal. For us, it was important that this difference was reflected in the building.

TG: **When I look at the BMW Central Building, I see affinities with your recent work in Rome, Strasbourg, Weil am Rhein, and elsewhere, as well as to earlier projects such as the Vitra Fire Station**

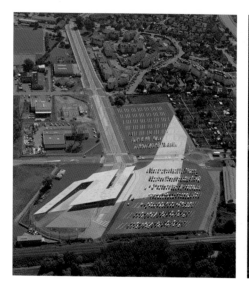

LEFT and RIGHT: Car park and terminus Hoenheim-Nord,
Strasbourg, France, 1998–2001

**and the Hong Kong Peak. How would you situate
this project in relation to your other work?**

ZH: This project is about making space through lines.
Like all of the projects you mention, it has to do with
the simple idea of people moving through a space. In
each case, that space derives from a linear process,
an exploration into the way a system of two-dimensional lines can devise a three-dimensional space.

In addition, we were determined to use engineering to create space. Structure in our work is not a
simple armature to support an abstract diagram; we
labor to deploy structural elements to heighten spatial
qualities. At BMW, a key device is the elimination of
columns. Here, as at the Science Center in Wolfsburg
(Germany), we worked closely with the structural
engineers to develop nearly column-free spaces.
This, of course, has a profound effect on the spatial
experience.

Topography and landscape also suggest alternative ways to deal with a large building. We have been

interested in ideas of landscape for some time,
stretching back to our work in Cologne and at the
Victoria and Albert Museum (V&A) and later in Rome
and BMW. The idea of the terraced interior at BMW
draws on our experiments at the V&A, and perhaps
also from spending so much time at Gund Hall at
Harvard. All of these experiences come to bear when
one develops a design.

TG: **In all of your buildings I find a very deliberate
choreography of spaces from the street into the
building. At BMW, when the landscape forms and
the showroom are completed, you will have constructed an entry sequence that begins well outside
the proper entrance to the building. Could we talk
about this project in terms of choreography and
context?**

ZH: I think this comes from years of training, of
studying composition, figure-ground, urban organization. We have been pursuing this sort of investigation

LEFT: Vitra Fire Station, Weil am Rhein,
Germany, 1990–94
RIGHT: The Peak, Hong Kong, 1983

for years; it is simply the way we investigate architectural space. From the beginning, we have been obsessive about diagramming context.

TG: Did these obsessive techniques develop out of your education at the Architectural Association (AA)?

ZH: There was never a definitive AA technique, but these ideas were certainly part of the discourse at the time. For us, context ceased to be about historicism or traditional contextual relationships. It became critical. This led to a series of advances in technique. We transformed the figure-ground as a method of investigation.

Also, after the '68 revolution, things collapsed. It was at this time that the social project erased the formal project. That, I think, was the end of modernism.

When I came to school at the AA in 1972, the place was antiformal, antidesign. Everything was a discussion about the city, and it was from this context

that the so-called paper architecture of the 1970s arose. That work was very important for thirty years, and its influence on the current situation is phenomenal. I think all of this happened because we had lost faith in modernity.

The other reaction to this loss of faith was, of course, historicism. Though many of its practitioners claimed their work to be contextual, it was actually just pastiche. Our work was a critique of these historicist fantasies. Of course, there was also the social project, the various drawing projects—these were our versions of contextualism.

Nineteen eighty-three was the critical year. In the span of one week, I was awarded the Peak competition and Bernard Tschumi won La Villette. At that moment, the AA's importance shifted. It was no longer a school that simply produced radical designs. Its teachers and students were now seen as capable of winning major competitions. Of course, Rem Koolhaas was also very important. His entry to the La Villette competition was a seminal project

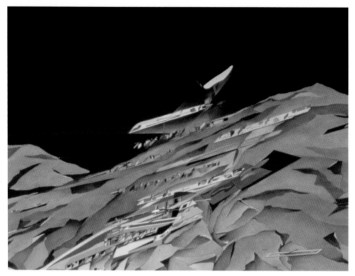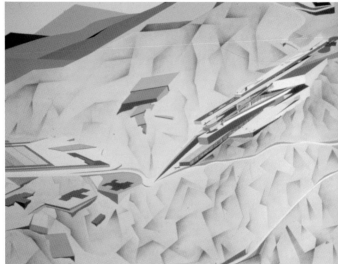

LEFT and RIGHT: The Peak

at the time, even though it was Bernard's entry that was built.

All of that work garnered a tremendous amount of press interest. That was the beginning of public interest in alternative fantasies for the city. But the historical project remained quite powerful.

TG: It is still powerful.

ZH: Not in Europe. Here, it has vanished. In London, perhaps you see it in a few schlocky developers, but in most cases, their ambitions have shifted from historicist and vernacular to pseudo-high-tech.

It took a long time to develop these projects, simply because there was no work. Through the 1980s, almost all of the available work was commercial—there were very few public buildings and very little housing. In this way, I find the U.S. and the U.K. to be similar—the dynamic is driven by economics, and the clients tend to be less adventurous. In the 1980s, I think there was a desire for a new

identity in the U.S., a desire to compensate for a perceived lack of history. The response was to adopt neoclassicism or postmodernism, which was easier. This was a very dangerous moment when rationalism, postmodernism, and classicism converged and became almost one.

TG: Were you reacting directly against these trends?

ZH: Not exactly. In my third year at the AA, I was a student of Leo Krier. It was then that I realized that I did not believe, as so many did, that the only way to move forward was to go backward. At that time, Krier had not yet embraced historicism. But in one year, he made the transition from a modernist/rationalist, whom I liked quite a bit, to a full-blown historicist.

TG: What happened?

ZH: I think he really believed in it. Regardless, I had a very positive experience with Krier. As a third year

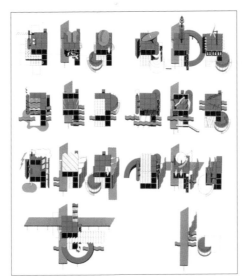
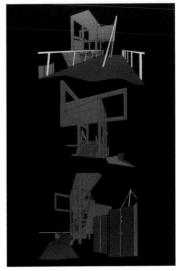

LEFT: Bernard Tschumi, Parc de la Villette, Paris, France,
1983, folly isometrics
RIGHT: Parc de la Villette, folly perspectives

student, I was engaged in large-scale urban projects, while most of my colleagues were doing tiny things, pavilions or whatever. My ambition was to understand the city, to understand urbanism through rigorous analysis.

During my second year, I studied typology. We would draw obsessively; we produced thousands of typological studies. By the end of that year, I could draw any plan imaginable. This obsessiveness produced a generation of professionally minded students. The work owed a debt to O. M. Ungers and his seminal research on typology. Ungers was also obsessive, and very clear. His work transformed everything.

After Krier, I joined Elia Zenghelis's studio. Zenghelis would come to Krier's reviews during third year. He was the only one who understood what I was trying to do, so I joined him. I did not yet know Koolhaas. He had just returned from the States, and was writing and lecturing about *Delirious New York*—it was an incredible experience.

In terms of my own work, I would say that after twenty years, an interest in fragmentation gave way to an obsession with fluidity. The move was not a break, but rather a continuous transformation. It was a slow transition away from Euclidean, ninety-degree geometries to other paradigms. I began to develop an interest in linear spaces, but not linear processes.

At the same time, I was determined to deploy the ground plane as a predominantly public domain. Over a series of projects, we began to multiply and transform the ground plane, which led to a series of investigations that had to do with the idea of terracing, topology, and landscape.

We were attempting to move away from the modernist ideal of a podium and a slab. For us, the surrounding landscape and the inhabited surfaces of the architecture were a continuous system. A seminal project for us in terms of these ideas was Düsseldorf. Here, we were obsessed with ideas of continuity and with proposing an alternative to the repetitive floors of the traditional modernist office building. Of

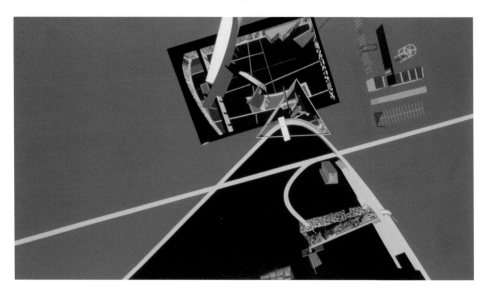

Irish Prime Minister's Residence, Dublin, Ireland, 1979–80

course, these ideas remain with us, and they are present at BMW.

These ideas were also present, in a less developed form, in our proposal for the Irish Prime Minister's Residence. Again, we worked to undermine modernist repetition—every floor was different. We were able to study this by developing what we called "x-ray drawings." These were composite drawings composed of a series of transparent layers that allowed one to see everything at the same time. It would not have been possible without having spent so much time drawing on Mylar and tracing paper at the AA.

We would first draw each component separately and then combine them into a single drawing. We worked to develop new ways of moving through space: rather than stack staircases as cores—the typical solution of modernist building—we would peel the various layers of the project and join them together. This resulted in a proto-fluid organization, a continuity of circulation that we continue to explore today.

In a way, the Irish house was a precursor to the landscape projects we have explored since.

Another important drawing was for the Dutch houses. Here, we were concerned with illustrating nonlinear connections, in developing new ways of drawing together parts of the city. Though these were projects for specific buildings, the focus was really on developing a response to the contemporary city, looking for new techniques for rebuilding the city. This was not the tabula rasa paradigm of modernism, but rather a project of juxtaposition and superposition as methods for inserting new interventions into an existing context.

TG: **And at BMW, where you were faced with a tabula rasa site, your intuition was to urbanize it.**

ZH: Yes, but continuity is crucial for a production facility. You cannot have a factory distributed over eight levels. In this instance, we are responding as much to our own obsessions as to the realities

LEFT and RIGHT: BMW Central Building, interior views

of automobile production. Though the project refers back to Fordism and the lineage of the assembly line, we wanted to create a new field of production.

PATRIK SCHUMACHER: The byline for BMW could be "articulated complexity." In the building, we attempt to deploy architectural language and formal discipline to organize a series of connections and to orient various flows—of people, of space, of automobiles—within a very large, deep space. The ambition was not to invent complexity, but rather to make apparent and clarify the complexities that were already inherent within the project.

We mapped the project's various flows as a series of linear diagrams. Translated into three dimensions, these linear flows become layers of bifurcating and intersecting trajectories, resulting in a layered space of movement with a strong emphasis on deep visual penetrations.

The architecture is characterized by key decisions made early in the project: We employed only homo-geneous, continuous materials such as concrete and welded steel; we strove to eliminate as many columns as possible; and we minimized the number of corners. Further, we attempted to have elements cross between levels as often as possible, producing a layered space in which one can trace the trajectories of our initial diagrams through varied elements in the project. The eye is drawn along continuous concrete walls; seamless, welded steel handrails; even the conveyor belts overhead. These lines flow in parallel, they bifurcate, they travel up and down through the section, but always tangentially.

LEFT and RIGHT: MAXXI National Center of
Contemporary Arts, Rome, Italy, under construction

One might call BMW a field project. Rather than work with a series of segmented, enclosed, and static spaces, we endeavored to provide a continuous, fluid space of movement. Here, the eye never comes to rest. As one moves around a corner, new vistas open up in all directions. In the best instances, it almost gives one a sense of flying.

Such a space calls for a different manner of orientation. In a static, compartmentalized space, one knows one's location by memorizing position—now I am in compartment A, now I move to compartment B. We rejected this kind of spatial experience at BMW. Instead, we worked to create a continuously differentiated space, a space structured by bundled, converging, and bifurcating trajectories.

BMW continues investigations begun in earlier projects such as the Contemporary Arts Center in Rome and the LF-1 project in Weil am Rhein. Each of these projects deals with the organization of a number of trajectories over different levels, with the complexity that arises from these trajectories crossing and intersecting, and with the spatial experience of moving through them. Conceptually, BMW is very similar to Rome, though the articulation differs.

TG: **In Rome, you appear very deliberate about maintaining the integrity of each line. Each U-shaped channel, as it moves along, remains intact. At BMW, on the other hand, you seem concerned with breaking down the integrity of each vector to create a single, layered space.**

ZH: Yes. Rome is about flooding the entire site with this system of lines. It is less layered, more about how these different strands lay over each other. At BMW, we are making an office building—the ambition was to make an open plan. By terracing this space, we were able to differentiate that open space, to bring a degree of specificity to the open plan. The idea is that one can spill through the building and flow into the adjacent buildings.

LFOne/Landesgartenschau, Weil am Rhein, Germany,
1996–99

PS: In either project, one will experience moments of spatial intensity in zones of convergence and overlap and moments of repose where these bundled trajectories branch apart. In Rome, we required more quiet spaces to accommodate the galleries, while at BMW we were able to amplify and celebrate the multiplicity of layered trajectories inherent in the factory and its processes.

These qualities are most intense at the entrance. The vectors from the car park are collected here, then fan out along various paths into the building. Above, the bridge element counters this inward momentum with a strong cross current.

Of course, all of this spatial agitation must accommodate program, and we endeavored to bring the same organizational principles to the task. To maintain the continuity of these trajectories, the open office areas were not partitioned in traditional ways nor were they treated as a continuous field of undifferentiated space. Rather, we developed alternative methods for articulating different areas. As the design

developed, opportunities for programmatic specificity presented themselves. This is perhaps most apparent in the series of terraces that constitutes the main office area. In other instances, a glass wall might complete a domain. That space would get a name and a discreet function, but we were careful never to interrupt the flow. Our planning strategy, then, was never an act of compartmentalization but rather a kind of soft zoning or territorialization.

There are a lot of things going on in the factory, which created a constant struggle against cluttering, against impediments to flow. Much of our work involved taming the chaos of elements and structures and infrastructures.

TG: **I think that is not only one of the great achievements of the building, but also its great irony. In the initial diagrams, the ambition was to tease out complexity in order to generate a rich and layered space. This was achieved through the multiplication, transformation, and agitation of** linear flows. This process transforms a tabula rasa site into a rich matrix of flows and intensities, effectively urbanizing the rural landscape.

But almost immediately, this process of amplifying complexity had to be reversed. The clarity of these initial diagrams is threatened by the myriad requirements of construction, structure, program, and so forth. The process of generating complexity very quickly became, as you said, a struggle for clarity.

To visit BMW and not have one's attention clamored for by sprinkler pipes, HVAC, signage, and all those workaday elements that undermine so many buildings is no small achievement. All of those elements are there, but each has been marshaled into alignment with the broader ambitions of the project. For me, that is the real achievement of the building. It demonstrates that it is possible for an architect not to throw her hands up in defeat in the face of the brute realities of construction.

LT: That is the hardest and most time consuming part of the process, actually.

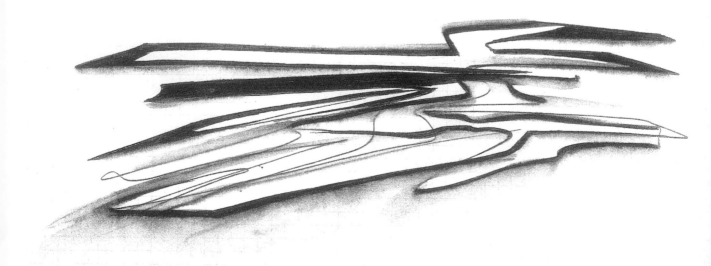

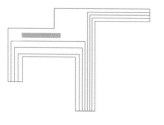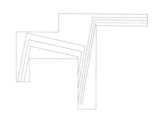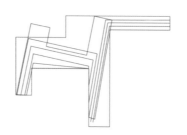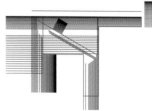

Preliminary vector diagrams

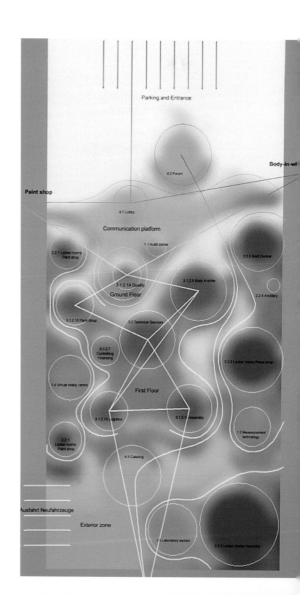

Preliminary diagrams
RIGHT: Preliminary program-analysis diagram

opposite: Preliminary bas-relief site model

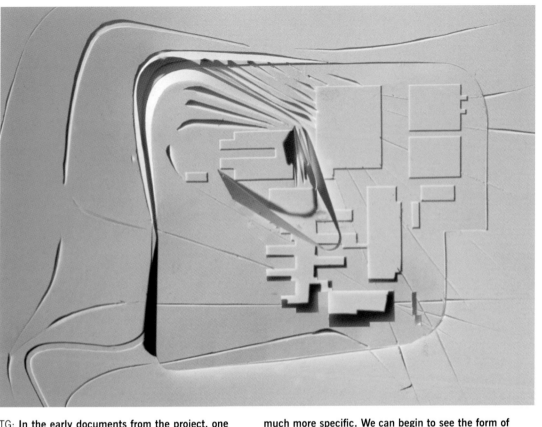

TG: **In the early documents from the project, one will notice two parallel investigations. On one hand, we see an abstract analysis, an attempt to make visible the latent forces within the site. On the other, we see fairly straightforward program analyses (see opposite). Were these operating independently?**

LT: At first, yes. We were attacking it from both ends. One investigation had to do with large-scale issues of the project—how to access the site, what a visitor will experience, which flows and forces might act as organizational vectors. The second investigation focused on the program brief, on what we were asked to provide, on how the building was intended to work. These early bubble diagrams (see opposite page right) helped us to understand BMW's ambitions. In the next step, we attempted to merge these two lines of inquiry into a single investigation.

TG: **How quickly did the two lines come together? In these illustrations (see page 28), the flows become**

much more specific. We can begin to see the form of the building and some of the landscape strategies. How is the program analysis informing these models?

LT: These studies were intended to help us understand what kinds of spaces were possible on this particular site. It was not an exercise in program distribution at this point, but rather a slow search for the general layout of the building. Once this began to take shape, we are able to begin assessing the size and location of certain functions. It was a slow process of simultaneously making sense of the form and the function. One should think of these studies as tests. Some of them are more formal, others more specifically functional.

TG: **What is that process like? Who is making these models? Who is talking about them?**

LT: We usually work in three or four media at a time. We always have someone in the workshop testing

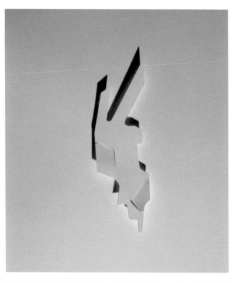
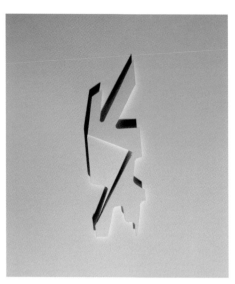

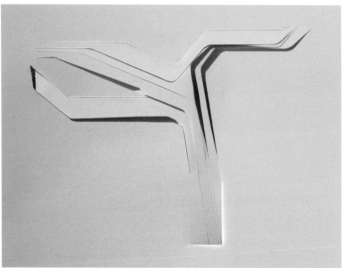
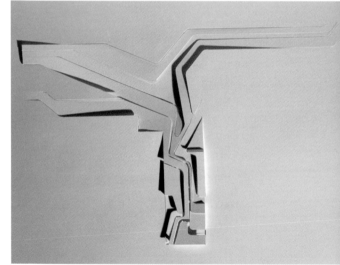

Preliminary bas-relief studies
RIGHT: Preliminary vector diagram

opposite: Preliminary site diagram

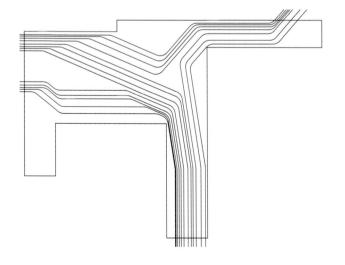

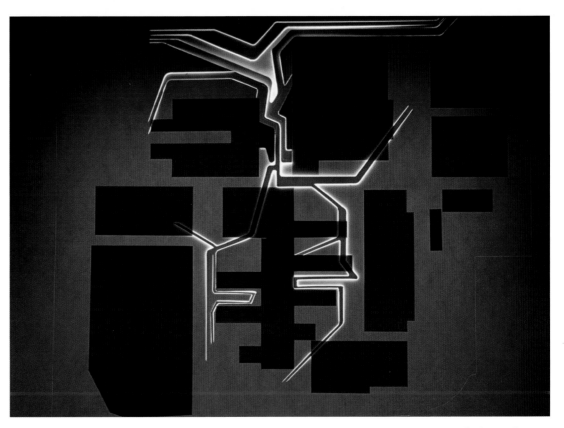

the ideas in physical models. At the same time, we will have someone developing 3D models in the computer, as well as people developing more traditional two-dimensional drawings. And of course there are many, many sketches.

Each medium has certain advantages and foregrounds certain tendencies. To work simultaneously in this way allows us to develop a range of possible interpretations of our ideas.

TG: **How big is that team?**

LT: In the early stages, it will be perhaps three or four people.

TG: **In addition to Zaha and Patrik?**

LT: Yes. Zaha and Patrik oversee all of the projects in the office, while most team members will work full-time on a single investigation. Obviously, as the project grows we have to add more people, but at the beginning, the group is fairly small.

TG: **This appears to be a very focused investigation. It seems possible, especially with a large team, that such a process would be in constant danger of losing focus. How do you maintain a consistent direction within the team?**

LT: Every few days, we all come together to assess the results. At that point, we will eliminate those things that appear to be headed in the wrong direction, and try to steer the team along the same course. This does not necessarily mean we limit ourselves to a single design but to a single approach. From there, we will spread out again and investigate further. It is a step-by-step process of generating materials and then trimming away what does not work. We meet fairly often as a team and at major milestones we will present to Zaha and Patrik.

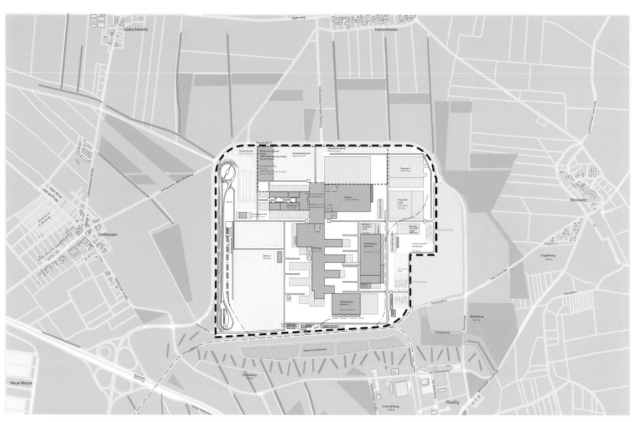

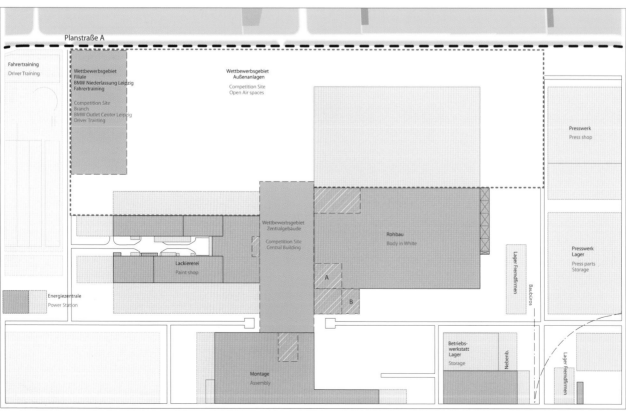

Planstraße A

| Fahrertraining | Wettbewerbsgebiet | Wettbewerbsgebiet | Presswerk |
| Driver Training | Filiale | Außenanlagen | Press shop |

Wettbewerbsgebiet
Filiale
BMW Niederlassung Leipzig
Fahrertraining

Competition Site
Branch
BMW Outlet Center Leipzig
Driver Training

Wettbewerbsgebiet
Außenanlagen

Competition Site
Open Air spaces

Presswerk
Press shop

Rohbau
Body in White

Wettbewerbsgebiet
Zentralgebäude

Competition Site
Central Building

Lackiererei
Paint shop

A

B

Energiezentrale
Power Station

Presswerk
Lager

Press parts
Storage

Lager Fremdfirmen

Bauburos

Betriebs-
werkstatt
Lager

Storage

Nebenb.

Lager Fremdfirmen

Montage
Assembly

Aerial view of plant under construction

opposite:
TOP: Factory site plan with surrounding context
BOTTOM: Site plan with immediate factory context

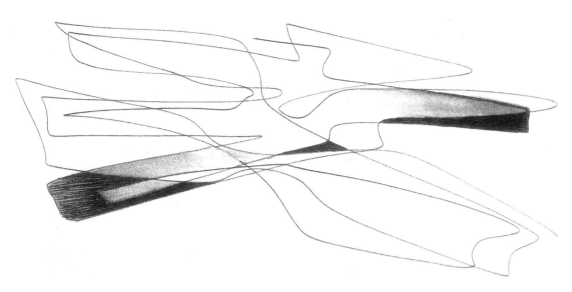

Preliminary sketch

TG: **Zaha's freehand sketches, though quite gestural, seem to resonate closely with the more specific models. Tell us about that relationship.**

LT: Our process works something like this: A competition will come along; perhaps we are invited to enter. The project architect will read through the brief, try to discern what the project is about, then he or she will go to Zaha to discuss it. Her initial ideas will often be expressed in a sketch. From the beginning, she will direct the process and guide our approach.

The project team works to translate those sketches, to test her ideas in terms of the project brief. This does not mean that the sketch will be explicitly represented in the project—the building will not necessarily look like the sketch. Rather, it should be thought of as a tool for expressing an idea.

TG: **How specific are these lines (see page 34, bottom left)? Each line is rendered identically, yet each represents a different flow.**

ZH: Yes, but this was simply our interpretation. We were trying to understand the forces of the project and use them to form the central space. Of course, such a process requires equal amounts of invention. One cannot analyze without invention.

TG: **How do you refine these lines? What propels these drawings through the various iterations?**

ZH: The diagrams start very early, perhaps even in another project. It is a very long process to develop a diagram. Often it has to go through three or four projects. Our projects usually begin with a sketch. But what I have in mind and what is interpreted by the office does not typically match—they would not understand what I was talking about.

LT: Yes, it often takes several attempts. But I think that is a good thing. Other ideas develop in these misinterpretations.

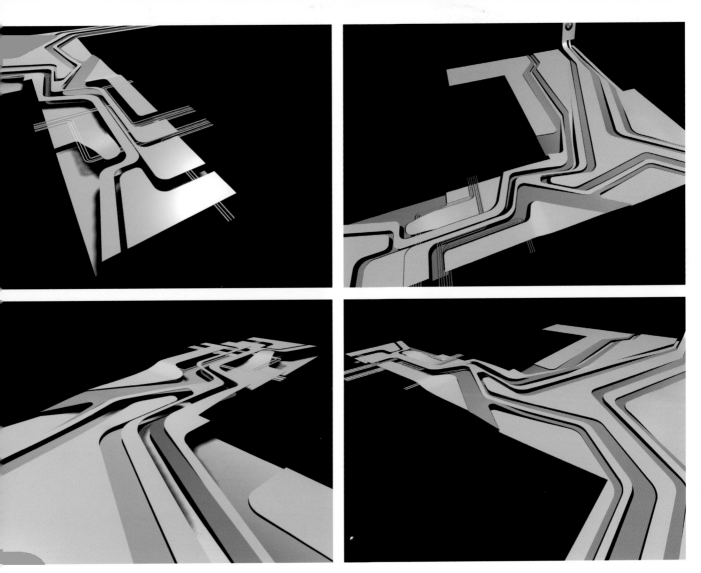

Renderings

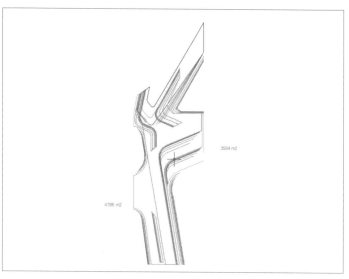

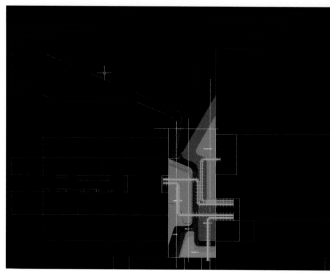

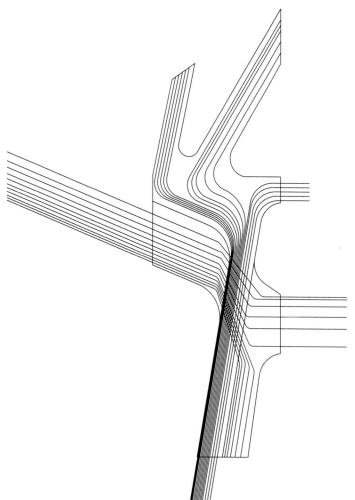

TOP LEFT: Stage-two plan diagram
TOP RIGHT: Stage-two program diagram
BOTTOM LEFT: Vector diagram
BOTTOM CENTER: Ground-floor program diagram
BOTTOM RIGHT: Upper-level program diagram

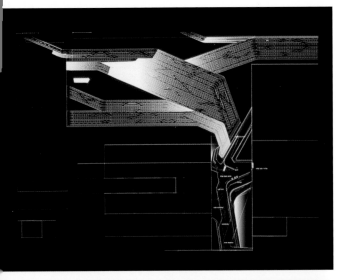

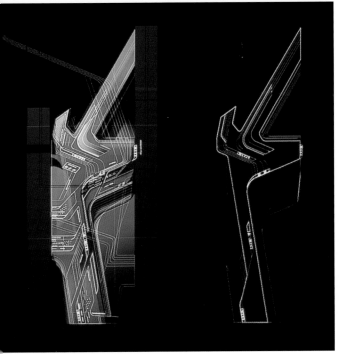

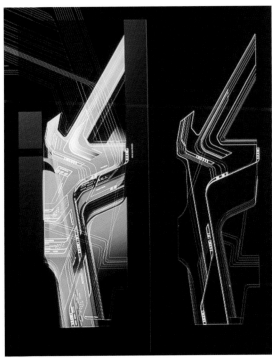

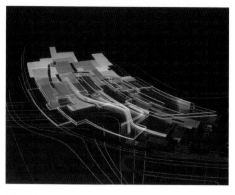 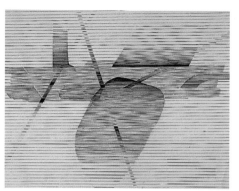

LEFT: Museum of Islamic Arts, Doha, Qatar, 1997
RIGHT: Illinois Institute of Technology, Campus Center, Chicago,
Illinois, 1998, preliminary diagram

ZH: I first did a diagram like this one for the Museum of Islamic Art in Qatar. It did not quite work there, but another opportunity arose with the competition for IIT. But it was not until the Rome project that the diagram really began to mature. And of course BMW represents another iteration.

**

TG: **By the end of the first stage, the building has begun to take shape. In many ways, the final version of the scheme is already apparent. How long did that process take?**

LT: In this case, we had about four weeks, five at the most. One has to move very quickly.

Obviously some of these diagrams and renderings were not translated directly into the building. Though the building does not look the same, I would not say that we abandoned these ideas. Rather, the ideas were reconfigured in the next stage. We discovered different ways to express them.

TG: **In the early studies, there are many lines at play. As the project progresses, it appears that many of these trajectories are distilled and combined to form the final building.**

LT: That is true. Just as with Zaha's sketches, we are trying to discern the essence of the idea. It is almost an archeological process of exposing those latent forces in the site. Through this process, we become accustomed to the forces of the site.

TG: **How did you make these ideas come across in the competition boards?**

LT: I think the key was to express our ideas of what the building should do. The first stage boards were still a bit vague in terms of the building proper. We had not yet developed the internal circulation; there

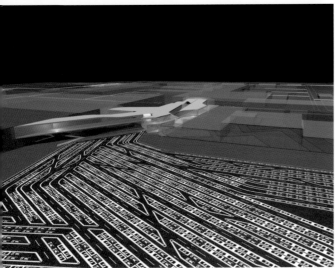

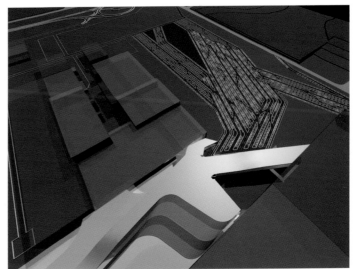

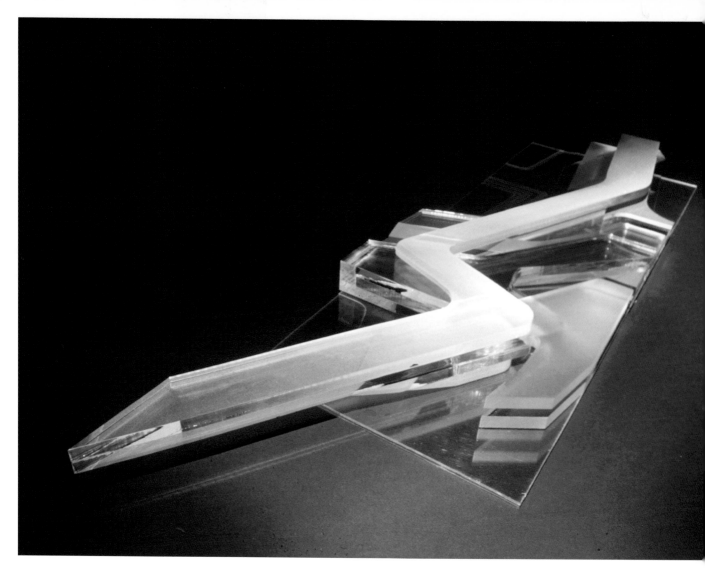

Final stage-one model

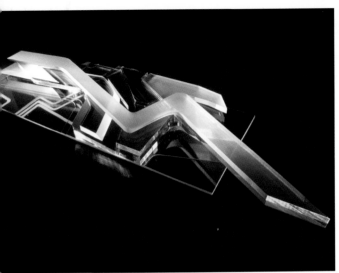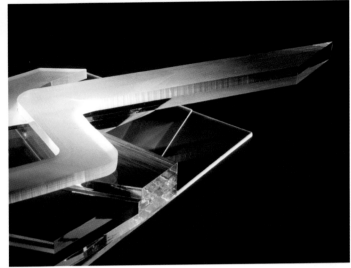

Final stage-one models

were no stairways or cores. It was simply an expression of what we felt the building should do, what kind of spaces we might offer, of what it might be possible to achieve.

TG: **It is crucial that a competition entry makes the project's ideas immediately graspable. How would you put those first stage ideas into words? What was the driving force?**

LT: I think it was about the connections of interior flows. The building was conceived as a connector between the various factory sheds. The building emerged from the diagrams of these connections. One of the main things that set our entry apart from the others was that we did not occupy the entire site. Many of the other entries chose to fill the entire area and then carve holes out of that mass. We knew from the start that we would not be able to afford to build out the entire site. Instead, we focused on the diagrammatic flows and only built where it was

necessary. This was a fundamental difference and I think the client understood. By conceiving the building in this way, we were able to provide a solution that was both central and continuous with the factory process.

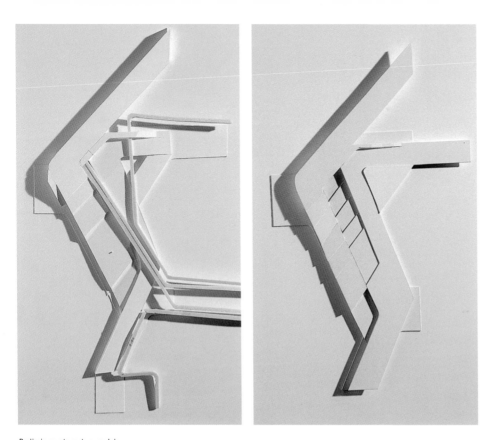

Preliminary stage-two models

TG: **Tell us about the second stage. At the beginning, we see a return to the initial bas-relief studies of the first round.**

LT: We had something of a breakthrough at the end of the first phase. Someone had made a little paper model—a quick three-dimensional sketch of the scheme. From that little model we discovered the essence of the project.

TG: **Where is that model?**

LT: It no longer exists, and it was never photographed. It was a tiny paper model that distilled the flows of the site. As we discussed the model, we began to bend the paper up and down and quickly realized a way that we could avoid the simple stacking of floors. We could treat the interior as a series of cascades and ramped surfaces that would touch down and connect the various levels. That was when the section idea appeared. We began to

explore two cascades that merged at a central level. Equally important were the series of meetings we had with the client during the second stage. Here, we began to discover what they were trying to achieve and how we could draw their ambitions into our design process.

TG: **The first stage jury comments exhibit some reservations about your initial scheme. Tell us about those.**

LT: BMW was very fond of the idea, but they were worried about its functionality. So as we developed the initial diagrams of the building form, we also began to explore much more specifically the programmatic workings of the space. These programmatic investigations helped us to distill the formal experimentation. We worked to boil down the first phase scheme to its essential elements. We labored to focus on those elements that were specific to the functioning of the space—everything else was eliminated.

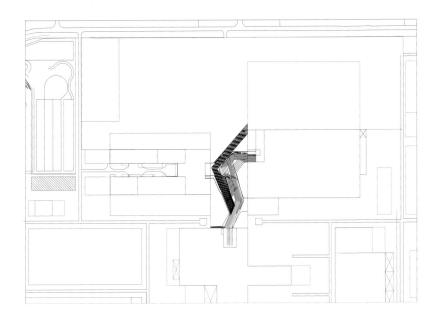

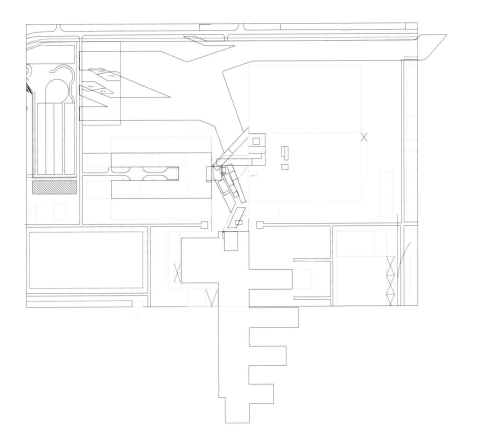

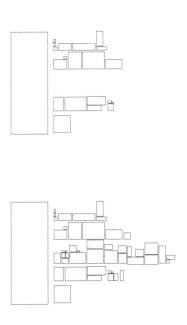

At the second stage, we knew that we had to submit quite comprehensive materials, so the size of the project team grew dramatically. This series (page 44) was an attempt to discern a structural coherence from the linear diagrams. As we were refining the building form in terms of programmatic accommodation, we began to think of it in terms of structure.

These investigations helped us to understand exactly how the project would work. At this point, we developed a series of large-scale models. Here we could study how the cascades would function, both structurally and functionally. There was a series of computer renderings that were developed at this stage as well.

TG: **How long did you have to complete the second phase of the competition?**

LT: I think it was six or seven weeks, and then one additional week to complete the model.

TG: **And how big had the team become?**

LT: By that point, it was a very large team. We felt that we had a good chance of winning, so we put in a lot of effort. At one point, we were up to fifteen, maybe seventeen people. We set up a single room in the studio as a base for the project.

TG: **Is it typical for you to devote a single space to a specific project?**

LT: It is very helpful to work this way, but it is not always feasible. Economically, we simply cannot afford to assign so many people to every competition we undertake. This particular entry was very demanding—it was a complex program with sixteen A0 (33.1 x 46.8 inches) panels required for the submission. But we felt we had a good chance, so we took a bit of a gamble. In the end it paid off.

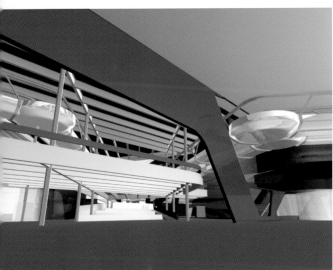

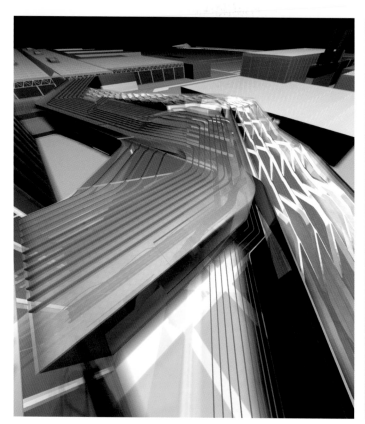

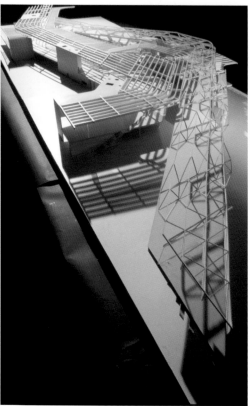

LEFT: Final stage-two rendering
RIGHT: Stage-two working model

TG: **Upon winning the competition, your aim shifted from winning to realizing the building. How did this change the dynamic?**

LT: Interestingly enough, it did not change our method much, though we almost completely changed the project team. All of the documents were to be produced in German, so we hired a few more German speakers. We won the competition in March 2002 and had to submit for tender that summer, so there was very little time to complete the construction documents. This was in a certain sense a good thing, as the short schedule did not allow the client much time for second guessing.

There was, however, one tense moment. As the factory sheds developed, certain program components that were originally part of our scope of work were moved out of the central building. We were constrained by a fairly tight budget, so BMW asked us to reduce the overall size of the building. There was no time to redesign the building from scratch, so we

Stage-two working model

began to look at squeezing and stretching the building form. This was, as you can imagine, terrible in terms of proportion—it would have completely ruined the project.

As we looked for a solution, we came to realize that the problem was not so much the size of the building, but rather the size of the site. With the reductions in program, our intervention was forced to stretch too far to make the necessary connections. To solve this, we suggested shifting the location of one of the factory sheds, effectively shrinking our site. This allowed us to make the necessary area reductions in both directions, maintaining the proportions of the scheme.

TG: **The contractors must have thought you were crazy to propose this.**

LT: At first, they looked at me as if I were completely nuts. But construction on the sheds had not yet commenced, so it was not a significant change to move it over. Three days later, they called to say they would alter the site plan. The factory shed was shifted one bay—eleven meters to the west. That adjustment saved the project from disaster.

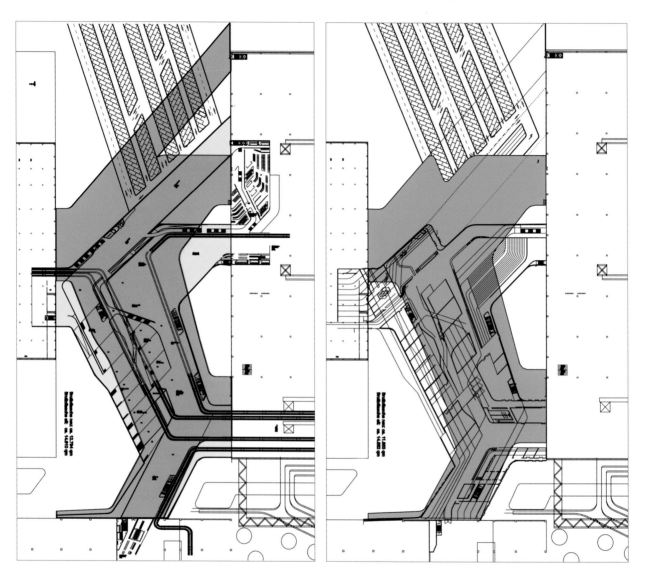

LEFT: Proportion study with reduced footprint
(orange), office floor. Original proportion in gray.
RIGHT: Proportion study with reduced footprint,
ground floor. Original proportion in gray.

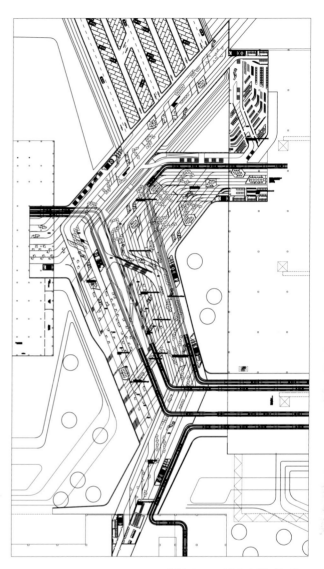

Original proposal (later built), office floor

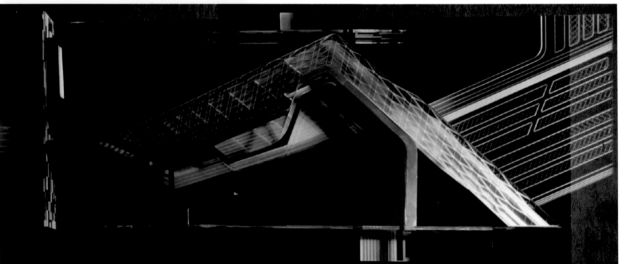

Final stage-two models

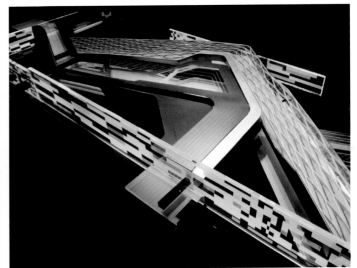

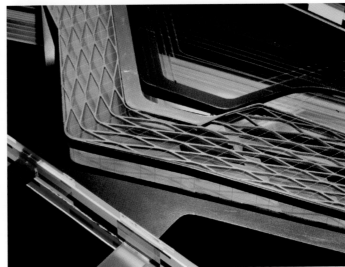

COMPETITION PANELS

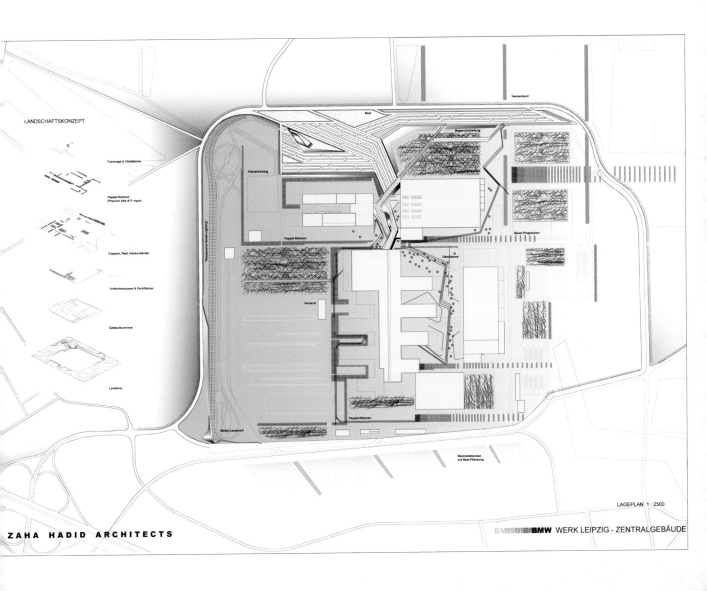

LANDSCHAFTSKONZEPT

Fusswege & Obstbäume

Pappel-Rahmen
(Populus alba & P. nigra)

Coppice, Reet, Heckenbänder

Anfahrtssequenz & Parkflächen

Gebäudeumrisse

Landform

LAGEPLAN 1 : 2500

ZAHA HADID ARCHITECTS

BMW WERK LEIPZIG - ZENTRALGEBÄUDE

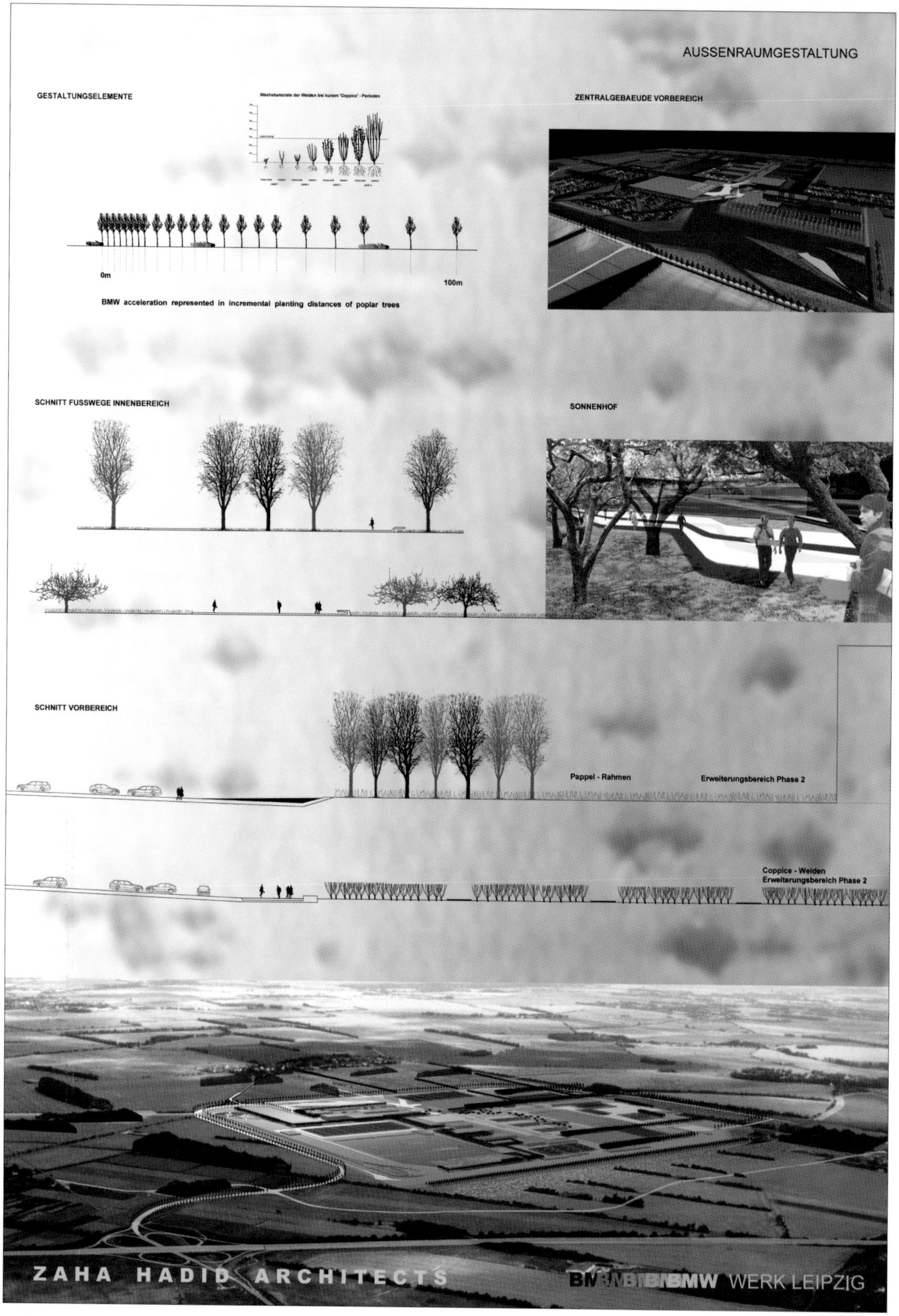

Competition panel 2, landscape eleme

previous page:
Competition panel 1, site plan (scale 1

AUSSENRAUMGESTALTUNG

GESTALTUNGSELEMENTE

Wachstumsrate der Weiden bei kurzen "Coppice" - Perioden

ZENTRALGEBAEUDE VORBEREICH

0m   100m

BMW acceleration represented in incremental planting distances of poplar trees

SCHNITT FUSSWEGE INNENBEREICH

SONNENHOF

SCHNITT VORBEREICH

Pappel - Rahmen   Erweiterungsbereich Phase 2

Coppice - Weiden
Erweiterungsbereich Phase 2

ZAHA HADID ARCHITECTS   BMW WERK LEIPZIG

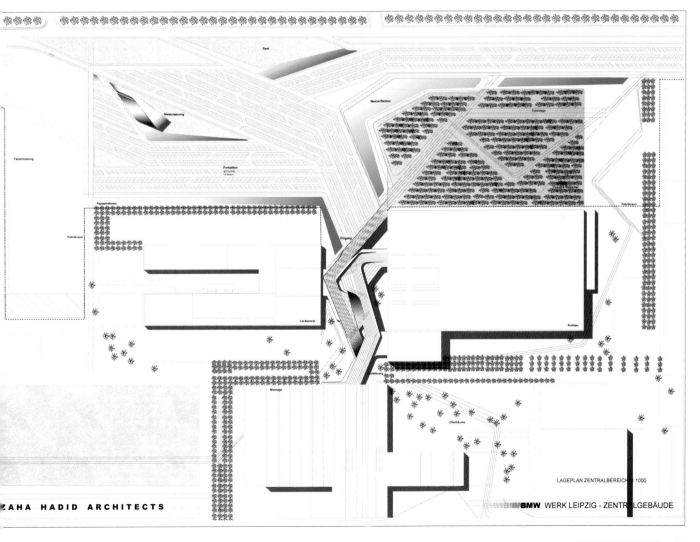

ZAHA HADID ARCHITECTS

LAGEPLAN ZENTRALBEREICH 1:1000

BMW WERK LEIPZIG - ZENTRALGEBÄUDE

ERDGESCHOSS 1:250

ZAHA HADID ARCHITECTS   BMW WERK LEIPZIG - ZENTRALGEBÄUDE

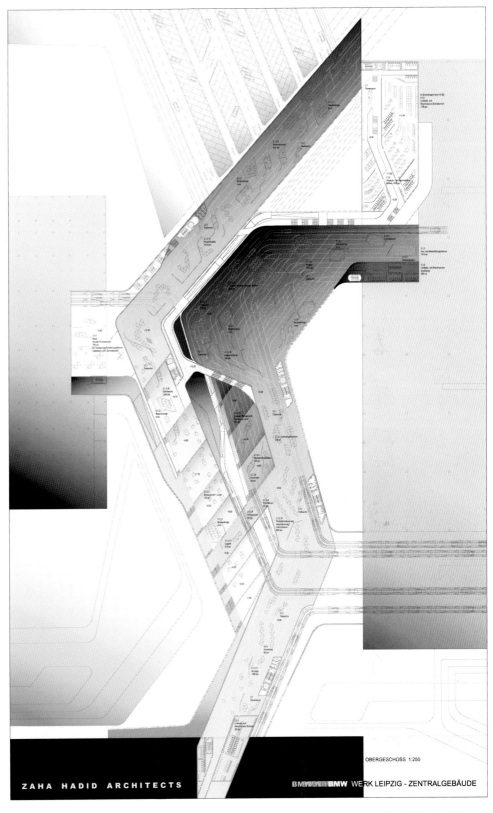

OBERGESCHOSS 1:250

ZAHA HADID ARCHITECTS

BMW WERK LEIPZIG - ZENTRALGEBÄUDE

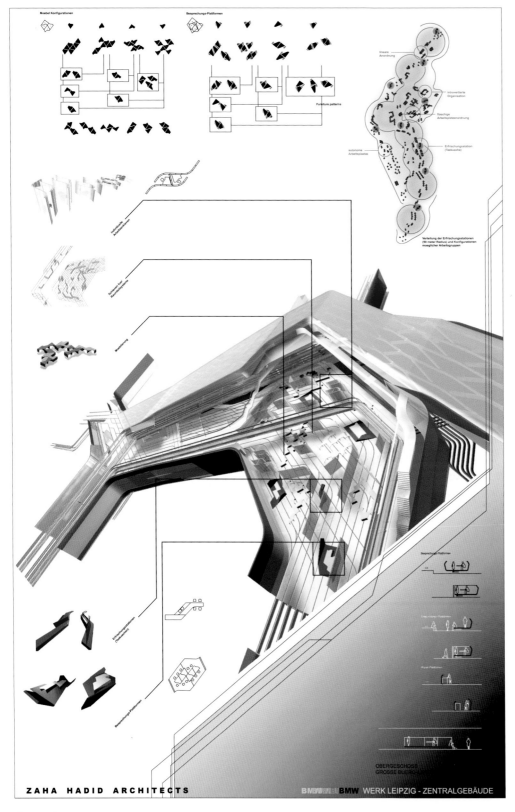

ZAHA HADID ARCHITECTS

BMW WERK LEIPZIG - ZENTRALGEBÄUDE

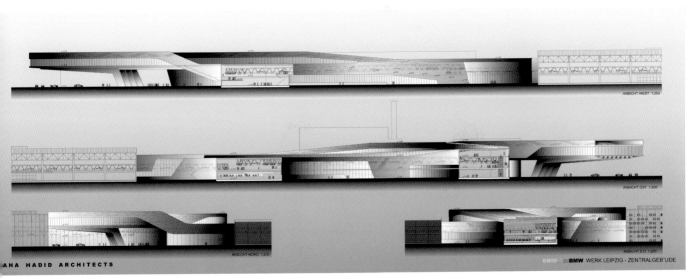

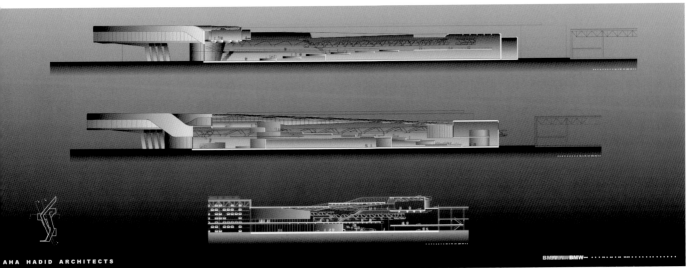

TOP: Competition panel 8, elevations
BOTTOM: Competition panel 9, sections

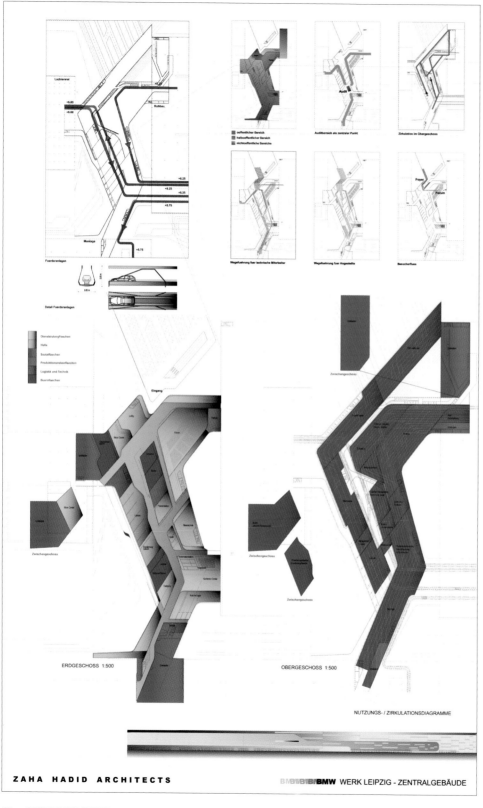

ERDGESCHOSS 1:500

OBERGESCHOSS 1:500

NUTZUNGS- / ZIRKULATIONSDIAGRAMME

ZAHA HADID ARCHITECTS

BMW WERK LEIPZIG - ZENTRALGEBÄUDE

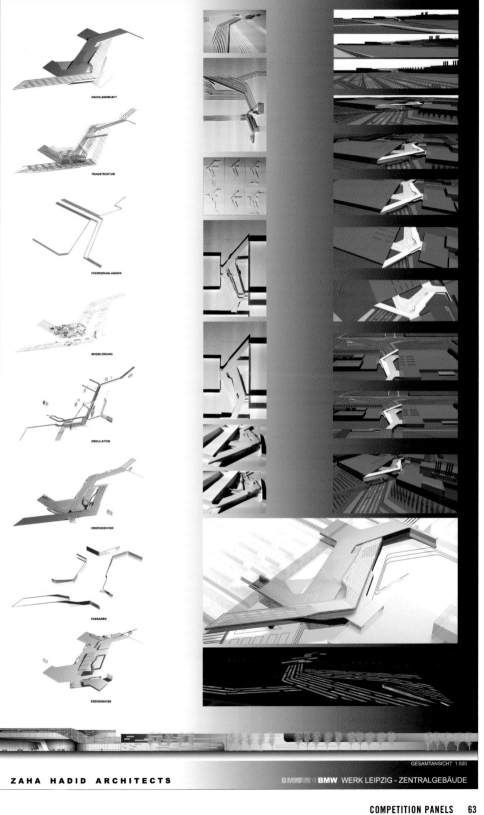

ZAHA HADID ARCHITECTS

BMW WERK LEIPZIG - ZENTRALGEBÄUDE

GESAMTANSICHT 1:500

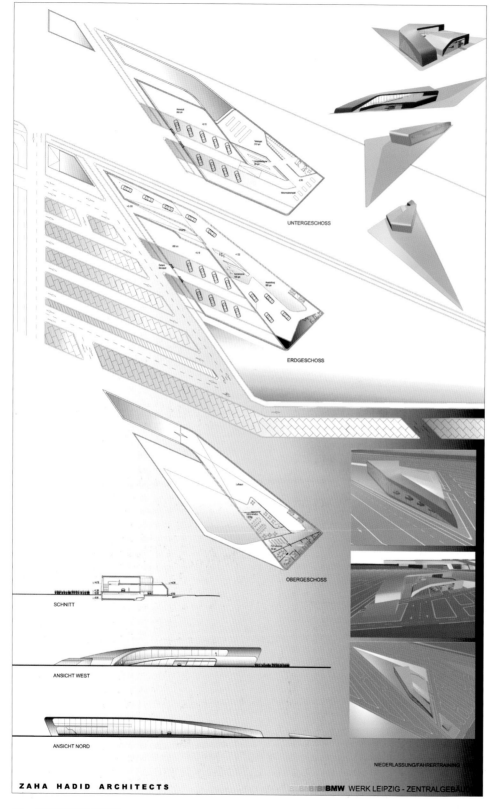

UNTERGESCHOSS

ERDGESCHOSS

OBERGESCHOSS

SCHNITT

ANSICHT WEST

ANSICHT NORD

NIEDERLASSUNG/FAHRERTRAINING

ZAHA HADID ARCHITECTS   BMW WERK LEIPZIG - ZENTRALGEBÄUDE

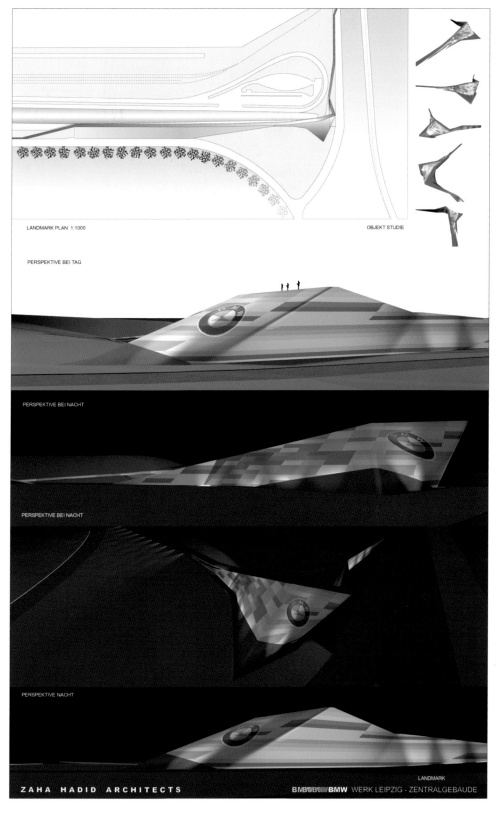

LANDMARK PLAN 1:1000

OBJEKT STUDIE

PERSPEKTIVE BEI TAG

PERSPEKTIVE BEI NACHT

PERSPEKTIVE BEI NACHT

PERSPEKTIVE NACHT

LANDMARK

ZAHA HADID ARCHITECTS

BMW WERK LEIPZIG - ZENTRALGEBÄUDE

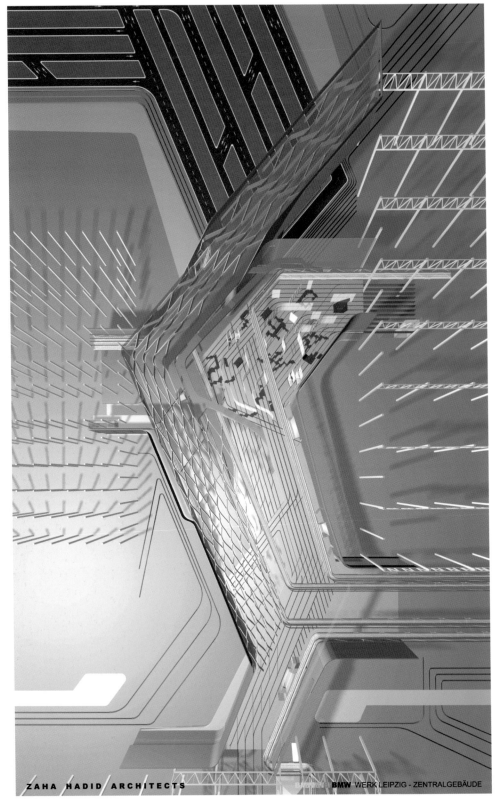

ZAHA HADID ARCHITECTS **BMW** WERK LEIPZIG - ZENTRALGEBÄUDE

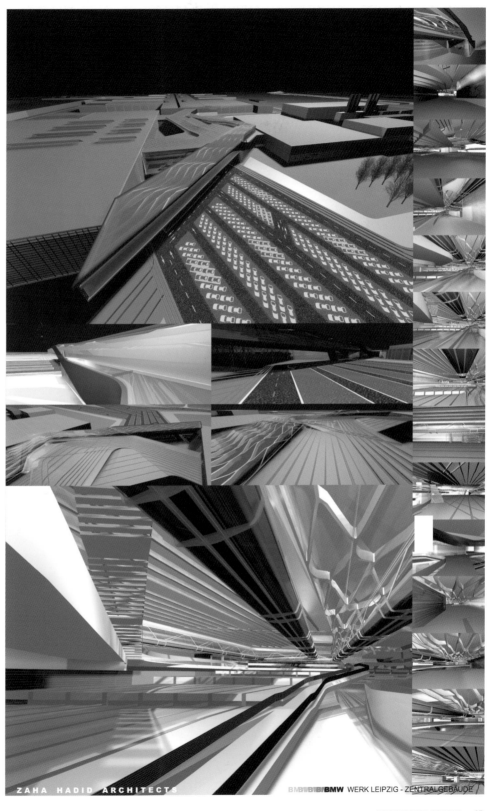

ZAHA HADID ARCHITECTS BMW WERK LEIPZIG - ZENTRALGEBÄUDE

DESIGN DEVELOPMENT

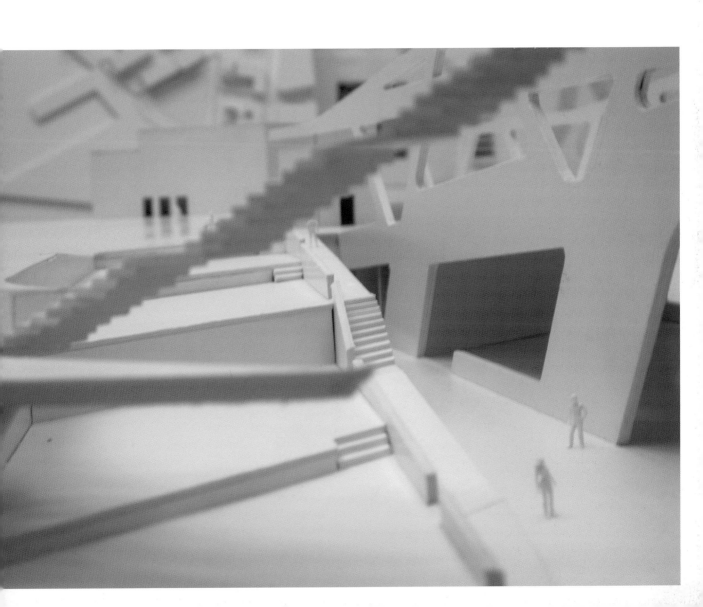

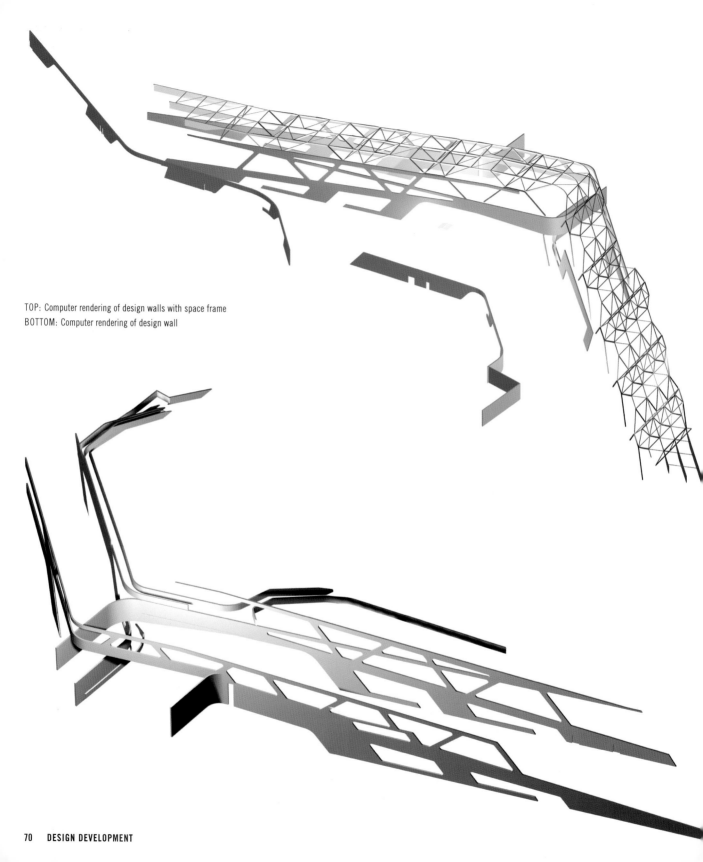

TOP: Computer rendering of design walls with space frame
BOTTOM: Computer rendering of design wall

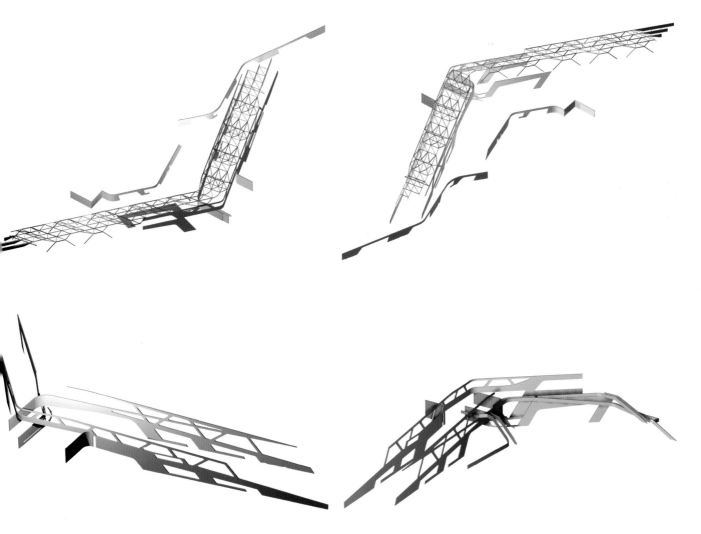

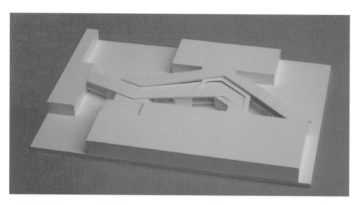

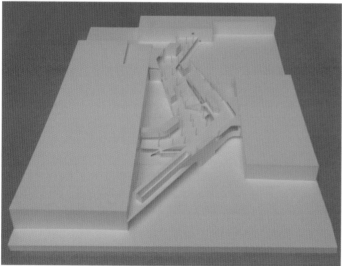

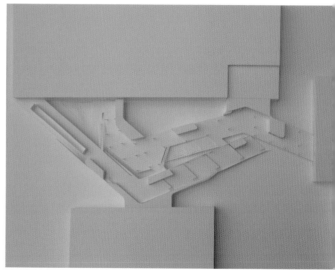

Design-development models (scale 1:500)

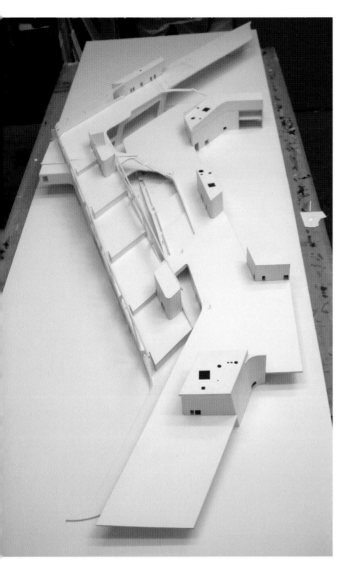

Design-development model (scale 1:100), February 2003

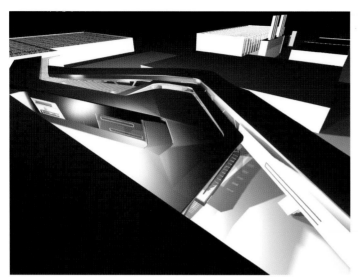

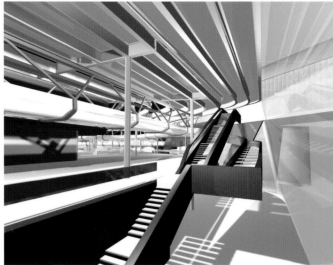

Design-development renderings

FINAL DRAWINGS

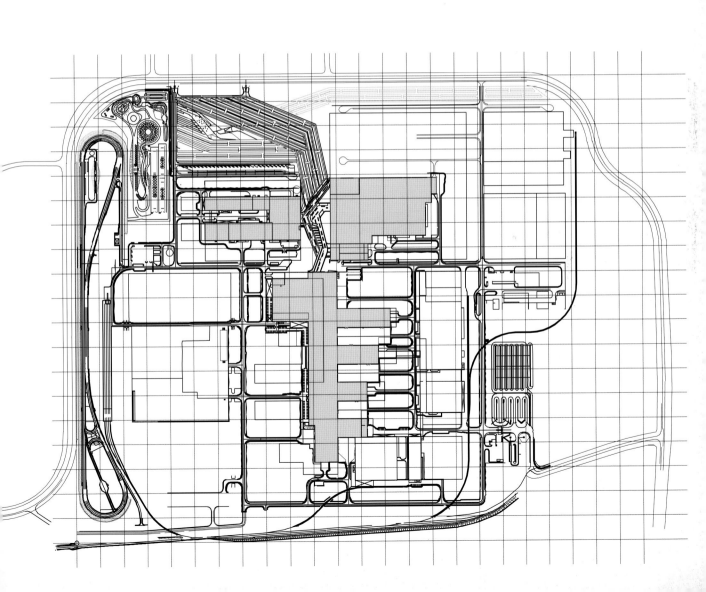

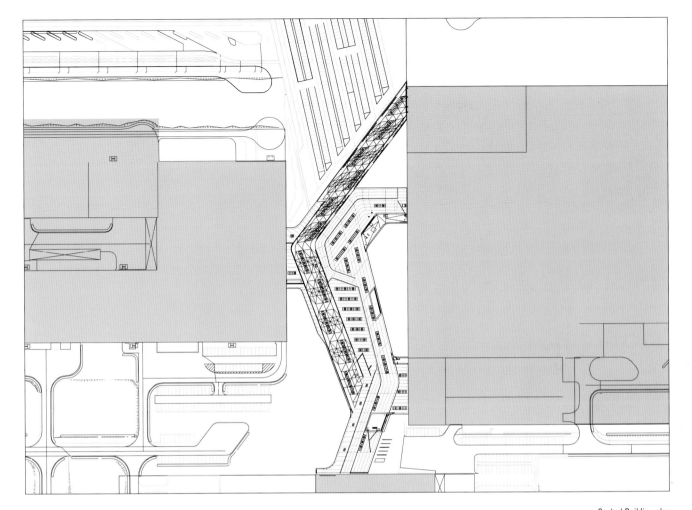

Central Building plan

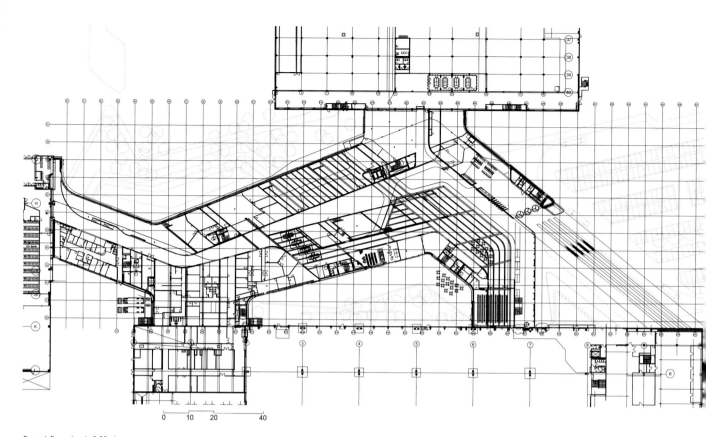

Ground-floor plan (+0.00m)

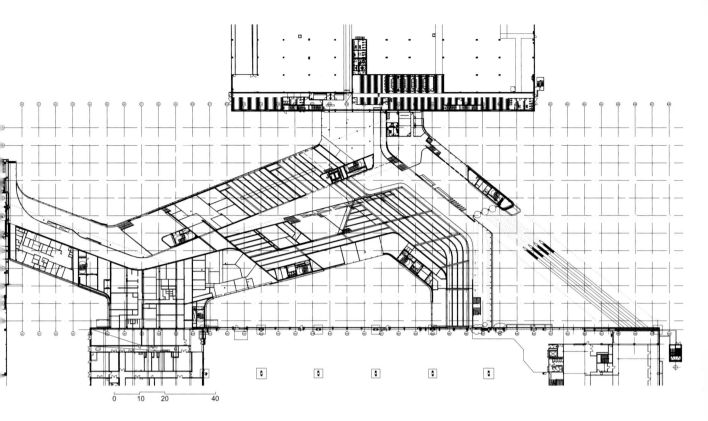

0 10 20   40

First-floor plan (+3.70m)

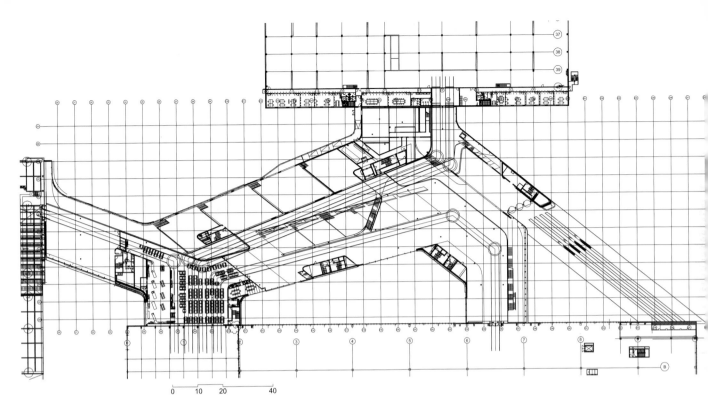

First-floor plan (+5.50m)

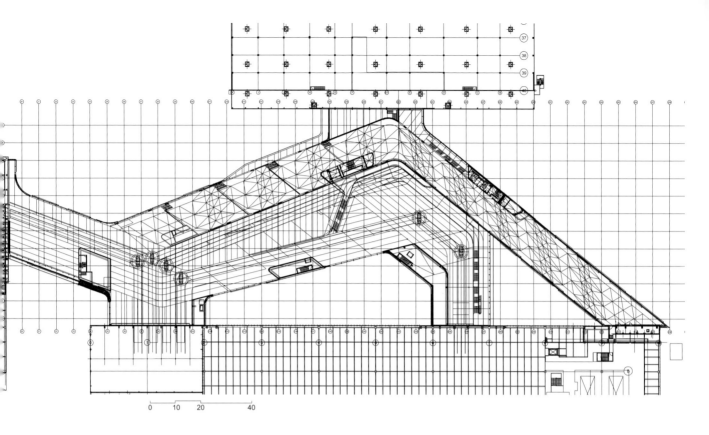

Second-floor plan (+12.20m)

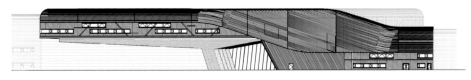

0 5 10   20

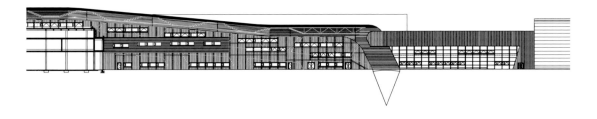

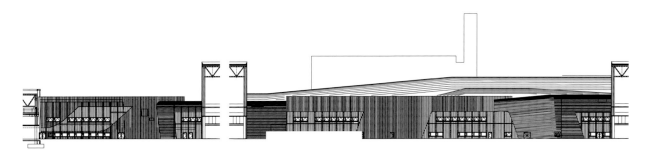

Exterior elevation

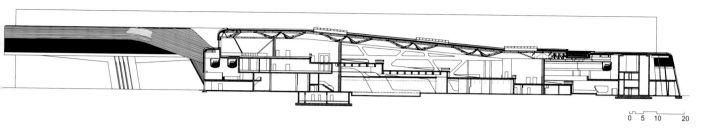

0 5 10   20

Building sections

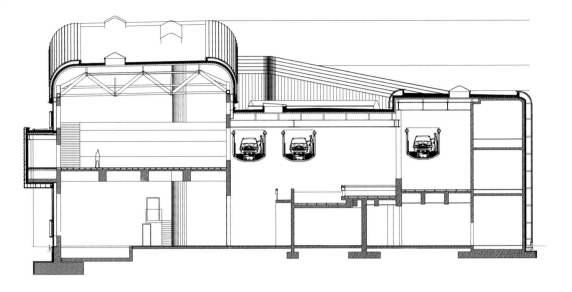

Building sections

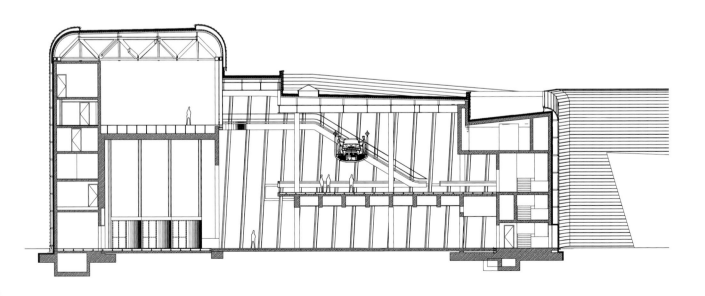

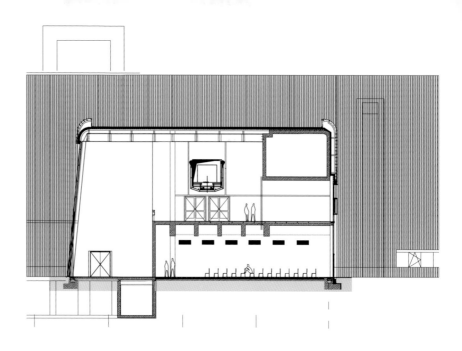

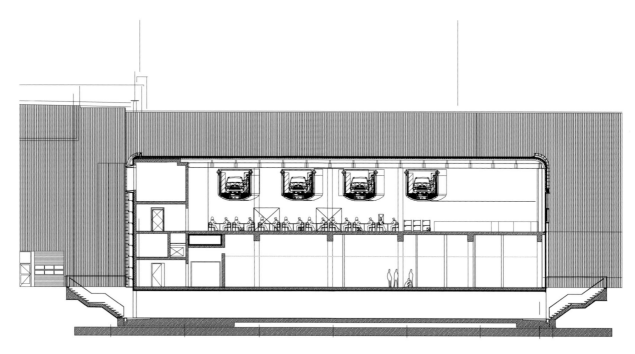

EXECUTION

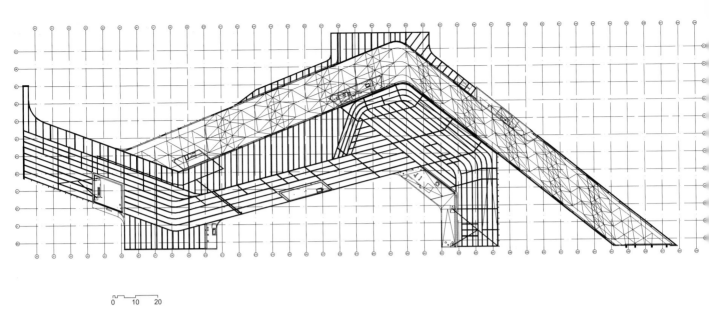

0 10 20

TOP: Roof-structure plan
BOTTOM: Roof-structure plan, detail

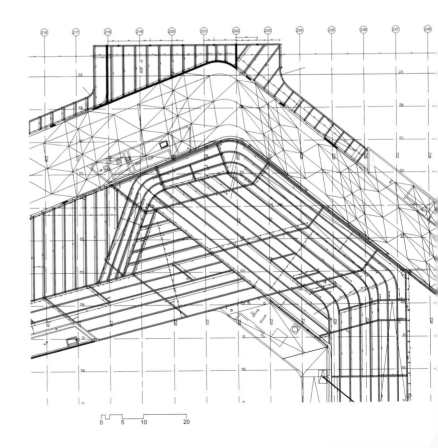

0 5 10 20

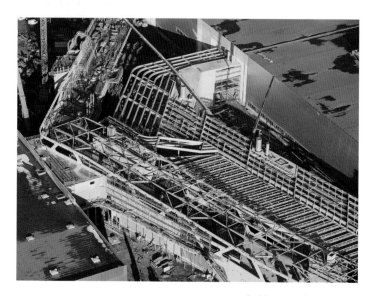

Roof framing under construction

TG: **Integration appears to be an important theme in this project, from the initial ambition of integrating the blue-collar and white-collar workers, to the blurring of boundaries between manufacturing and administration, between building and landscape, between various structural systems.**

ZH: Our ambition at BMW was to urbanize the site. As an urban phenomenon, it could not remain within the language of the factory sheds and the production lines. By adding a small public component, the project takes on a far greater degree of complexity.

But the project is about far more than these initial diagrams. One must quickly devote attention to the straightforward problem of making the building work, both in terms of program and in terms of structure. Engineering becomes critical in this regard—it becomes a potent means for making space. If one would simply attempt to build these diagrammatic ideas in a normative way, one greatly restricts one's ability to impact the spatial quality of the project.

Engineering offers the possibility to liberate space, to solve building problems in a new way. The crucial element is the way that one combines possibilities of engineering with the ambitions of the diagram. Some architects will build a diagram with no understanding of the structure. They may have an interesting spatial diagram, but the expediencies of construction will fill that space with columns, and the spatial experience they were pursuing will be lost.

We have always looked to engineering for ways to reinforce and enhance the spatial ambitions of our work. Even back to the days of the Peak, we searched for new ways to build. We found some in civil engineering.

After we won the Peak project, everyone told us that it could not be built. But when we turned not to traditional structural engineering but to civil engineering, new opportunities became available. The techniques employed to structure highways and bridges could easily be deployed to develop buildings. The engineering to achieve these projects

LEFT: Design-development rendering
RIGHT: Roof framing under construction

was available; we simply had to move beyond the conservative attitudes that traditionally pervade architecture and building construction.

TG: **How did the structure develop at BMW?**

PS: All of the structure was oriented to trace the lines of movement through the building, to emphasize these linear trajectories. Normally, the most efficient structural system will span the shortest distances. In this case, such a method would undermine the logic of the building, so we developed structural solutions that would exploit the long span. You will notice many instances where the steel roof beams are curved to follow the flows. These are not the most efficient ways to span these distances, but as the structure is such a major component of the visual field, we felt it necessary that it work beyond its role as support to become an orienting device within the space.

LT: In addition, we knew that we wanted to provide extensive glazing in the roof in order to bring natural light into the building. The space-frame roof was a way to maintain the directionality of the space as well as provide a lightweight structure to support the roof. It also helps us to eliminate columns within the space.

This is always an aim in our office. In a building of this size—295' x 950' (89 x 290 m)—it is impossible to eliminate all the columns, but our aim was to reduce their number to the absolute minimum.

TG: **I think this also speaks to our initial discussion of the differences between a modernist expression and a twenty-first-century interpretation. The march of the grid in a modernist building has to do with the underlying abstraction and stasis of the modernist plan. This project is conceived primarily in terms of movement—a grid of columns would be antithetical.**

Completed roof framing

Interior construction view with roof framing

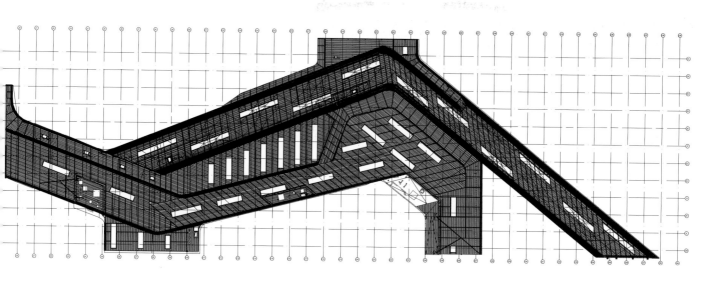

TOP: Roof plan
BOTTOM: Roof plan, detail

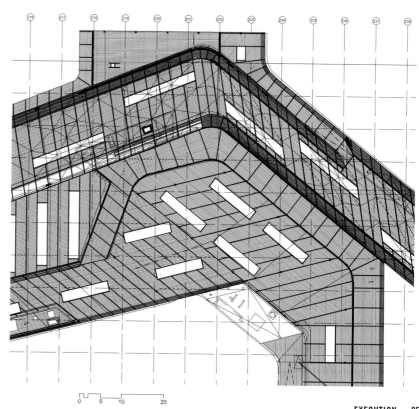

TOP: Installation of roof deck
BOTTOM: Aerial view of central building

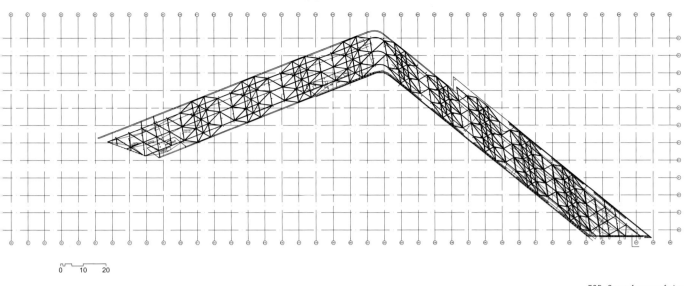

TOP: Space-frame roof plan
BOTTOM: Space-frame rendering

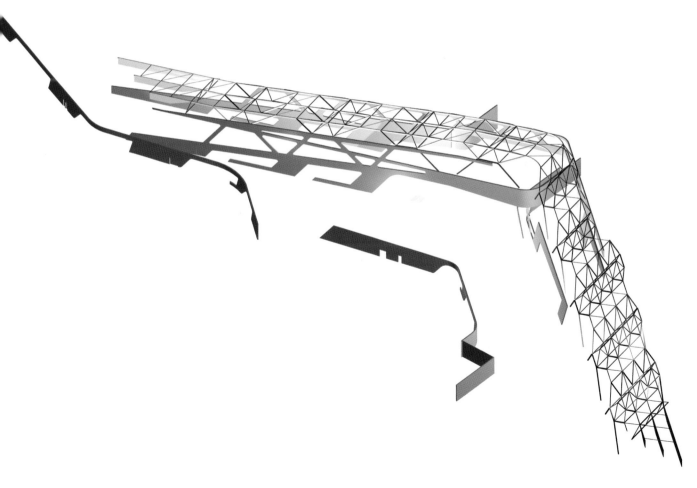

Space-frame assembly

 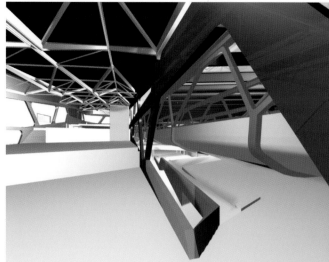

LEFT: Interior view with space frame
RIGHT: Design-development rendering

opposite: Interior view with space frame

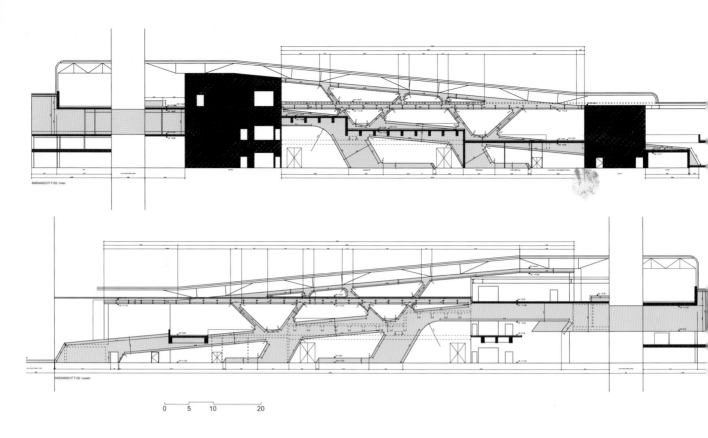

Interior elevations

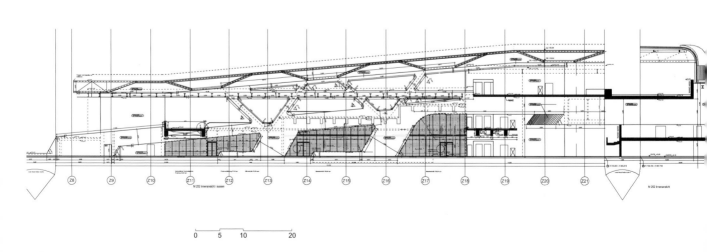

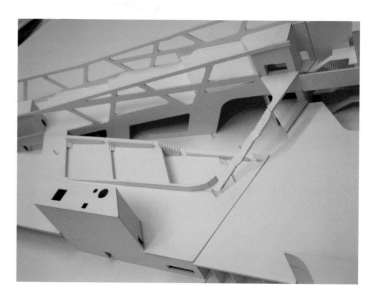

Design-development model

LT: You are right. In many ways, I think the grid is a thing of the past. You will notice in our construction drawings a traditional grid, but it has no bearing on the constructional logic of the building. Twenty years ago, every building would be reduced to a grid in order to be built. Here, that grid is solely a means of orientation in the drawings.

TG: **Another unexpected tectonic solution can be seen in the concrete walls. How did these elements develop?**

LT: In the first stage of the competition, we were not looking very closely at the structural system. We knew that we would eventually have to consider it, but at that stage, we were much more concerned with the spatial diagram. At the second stage, we began to consider much more carefully the way loads would be carried down through the building. The concrete walls became a way to combine and condense many different aspects into a single

element. The concrete walls could be much stiffer, they could carry more loads, and we could cut openings through them as needed. In addition, the diagonal elements provide better lateral support than a vertical column. The wall stabilized itself; there is no need for additional bracing.

PS: These walls stretch several hundred meters through the building, and climb vertically over several levels. Near ground level, they appear very solid but as they move vertically through the space, a series of cuts morphs the walls into a sort of truss at the top.

**

TOP: Pouring concrete
CENTER LEFT: Concrete formwork
CENTER RIGHT: Rebar installation
BOTTOM: Concrete formwork

TOP: Concrete walls under construction
BOTTOM and OPPOSITE: Interior views of completed office areas

TOP LEFT: Space for concrete stair
TOP RIGHT: View of concrete stair under construction
BOTTOM: Concrete-stair plan and section

opposite:
Views of concrete stair

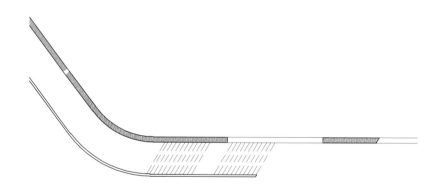

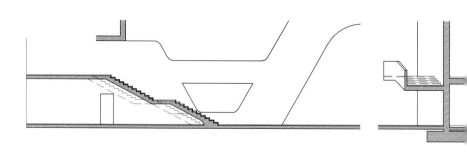

0   5   10   20

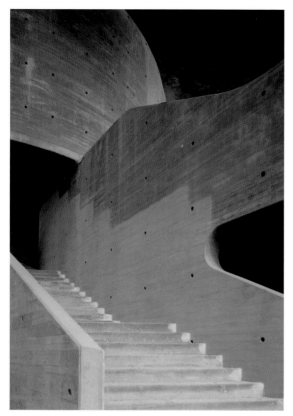

TG: **Another important component of the project is the system of connecting stairways. How did those develop?**

LT: The building was organized as a series of cascades. To rely only upon these linear circuits for building circulation would have led to certain inefficiencies, so we introduced a system of shortcuts. These shortcuts were crucial to the internal function of the space.

TG: **When the stairs occur at the edge of the cascades, they remain conceptually a part of the slab and are constructed in concrete. The shortcut stairs, on the other hand, introduce another system of circulation that is signaled by a material shift to steel.**

LT: Exactly. The concrete stairs were conceived and built as integral to the slabs, while the steel stairs were hung from the structure above. These steel stairs develop out of the steel balustrades that define the edges of the slabs. This continuity binds together the various slabs and also provides a subtle means of differentiating various zones with the space.

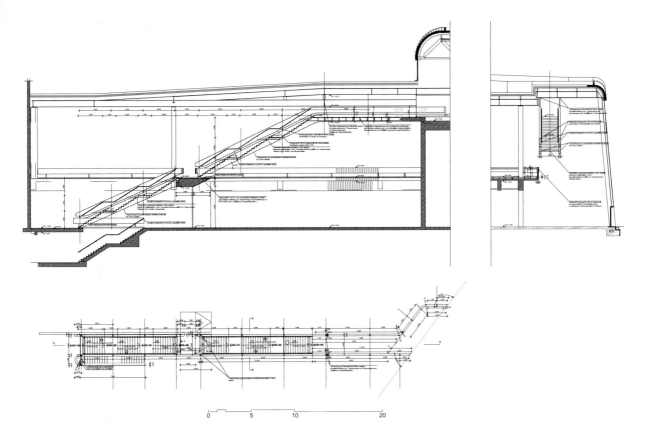

Steel-stair plan and sections

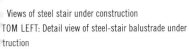 Views of steel stair under construction
TOM LEFT: Detail view of steel-stair balustrade under
truction
TOM RIGHT: Completed steel stair

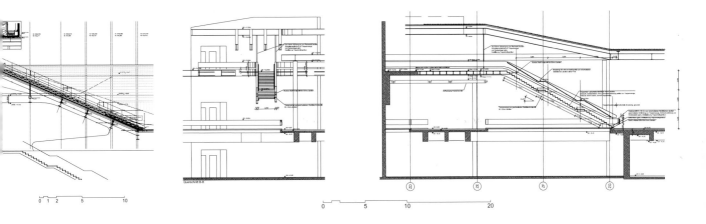

LEFT: Roof-stair section

CENTER and RIGHT: Steel-stair sections

TER: Steel balustrade, plan and section

OM: Stair in cascade, plan and sections

site:

Views of steel stair under construction

TOM: Views of cascade under construction

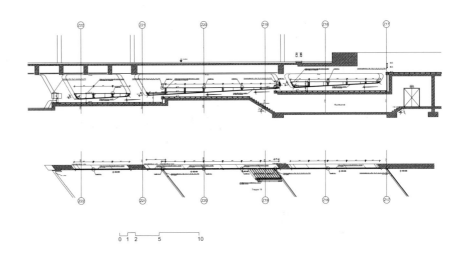

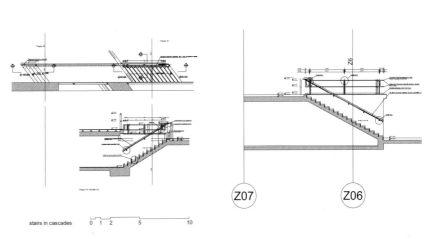

stairs in cascades

TOP LEFT: Design-development rendering
TOP RIGHT: Interior view with car conveyors
BOTTOM: Car-conveyor details

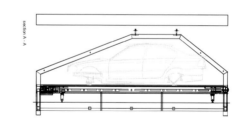

section A - A

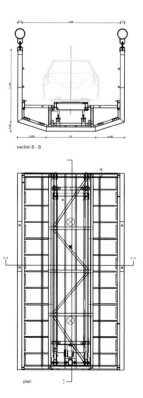

section B - B

plan

detail conveyor   0 0.5 1

LEFT: Car-conveyor joint under construction
RIGHT: Car-conveyor joint

TG: **And the car tracks?**

LT: It was given in the project brief that the cars would have to cross the site, though it was up to us to determine how this would happen. As with the other flows on the site, we were determined to make the cars that traversed the site a significant element in terms of spatial definition.

In the beginning, we were not sure if it was even possible. Not only were there acoustical concerns but issues with the manufacturing process. The engineers had to test that dust in the space would not affect the car bodies, that grease from the kitchen would not pose a problem for the unpainted chassis.

TG: **Ironically, these elements that were acoustical concerns from the beginning actually work to cut the reflectivity of the space through their perforated cladding. What one would expect to be an acoustical problem actually acts as a baffling treatment.**

Aerial view of entry canopy from car park

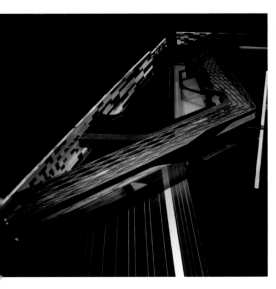

LEFT: Aerial view of model at entry
RIGHT: Model view of entry

TG: **One aspect of the competition schemes that was not realized is the penetration of the central building into the factory sheds (see plans, page 51). Why did this change?**

LT: That connection was initially made with the locker rooms, and their inclusion in the central building was part of the initial project brief. We felt that it made sense for the lockers to act as the transitions between the central building and the factory sheds. They would help to merge the two components and make continuous the functional workings of the building. Unfortunately, these elements were lost in later stages. BMW decided that the lockers should be located elsewhere. Another unfortunate change happened at the second floor. The so-called bridge element at the building entry was initially connected through the factory shed back to the first floor. This resulted in a complete circuit and greater integration between the central building and the adjacent factory. In the end, this did not happen, which was a bit of a pity.

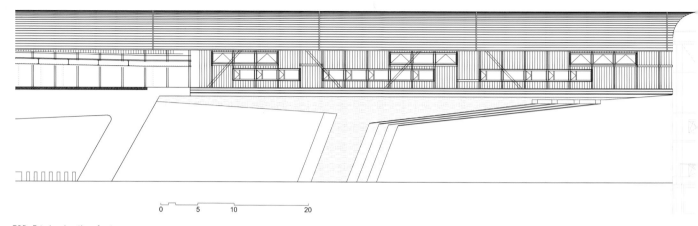

TOP: Exterior elevation of entry
BOTTOM: Bridge-reflected ceiling, plan, elevation, and section

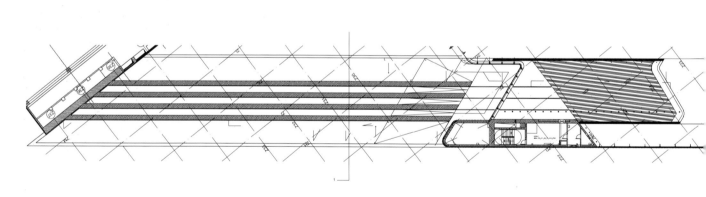

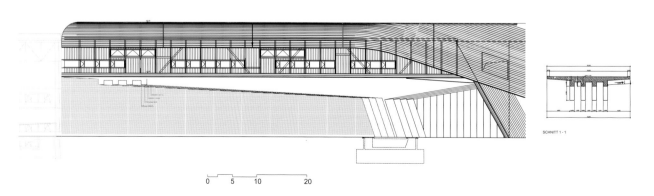

SCHNITT 1 - 1

TOP: View of entry canopy under construction
BOTTOM: View of completed entry canopy

TOP right: Views of entry canopy under construction
TOP left, BOTTOM and OPPOSITE: Views of completed entry canopy

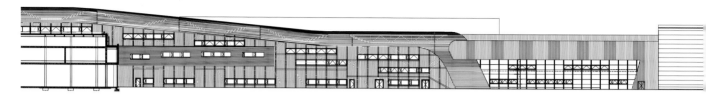

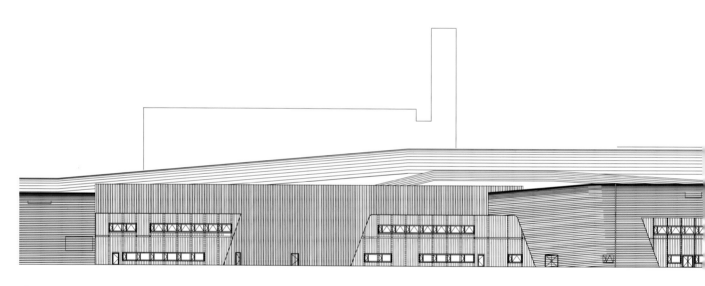

Exterior elevations

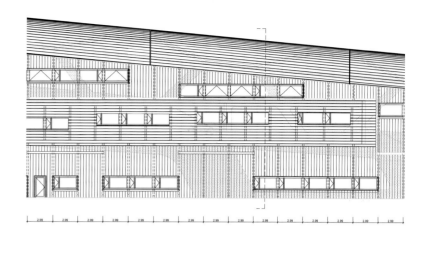

Elevation detail

TG: **BMW clearly builds upon many of the investigations and obsessions that have concerned the office for some time, but I'm not sure that it is the culmination of those investigations. What did you learn from the project? Are there unanswered questions, issues raised that have begun to inform current work in the office?**

PS: I don't think the project is a culmination either, I'm sure we will continue to investigate these issues. As far as new questions, this project forced us to address issues of cladding. By employing cast-in-place concrete as the dominant material at Wolfsburg, Vitra, and other earlier projects, the issue of cladding was suppressed. Here, we engaged it directly. In certain parts of the building, I think it works very well. At the building entry, for example, I find the cladding very elegant. But in other areas, in some of the courtyards, the clarity breaks down, and the results are less satisfying.

The issue is one of composition—the facades take on the character of the initial line diagrams with which we began the project. At the entry, these striations occur across all the different materials at play. Bringing the continuity and striation of the initial diagrams to bear on a composition of steel, glass, and concrete was an interesting exercise that we will certainly explore again in the future. So that is something we learned and will continue to work on. We are obsessed with the question of how to resolve a complex geometry in architectural form. Beyond our own investigations, we pay careful attention to the experiments of our colleagues. For example, I find Frank Gehry's Bilbao, for all its groundbreaking achievements, to be somewhat overburdened and unresolved. For me, it does not work. At the Disney Concert Hall in Los Angeles, the result is more successful, but I don't feel that Gehry has yet solved the problem.

At the other end of the spectrum, one might consider the work of Norman Foster. Here in London,

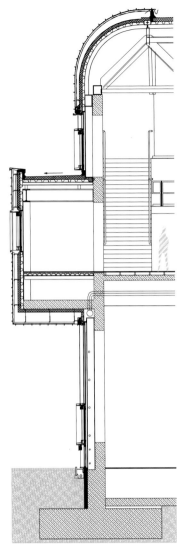

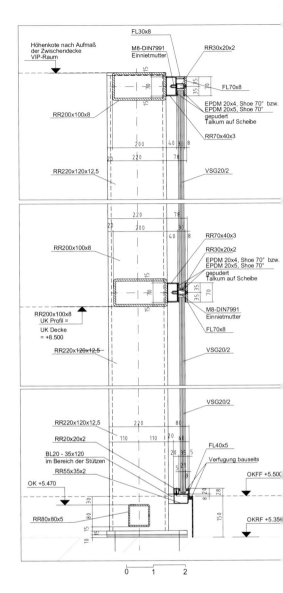

LEFT: Interior glazing details, facade section
RIGHT: Interior glazing details

we can compare his Swiss Re Headquarters tower to London City Hall on the south bank of the Thames. At City Hall, each curved panel had to be distorted a bit differently. Every joint, every handrail, nearly every element in the building has to be slightly distorted. Here, you will find an obsessive attention to working out the detail, but again, I don't think it quite works.

TG: **I agree. For all the obsessive articulation at City Hall, I do not find the result to be very elegant. But all of these projects represent concerted efforts to work out a pressing issue in contemporary architecture. And in each case, we have focused not on the overall form, but rather on its execution and detailing.**

PS: You are right, it is in the detailing that these projects succeed or fail. And that process can get very expensive.

TG: **What about materials?**

ZH: It seems that we have done all of our work in concrete. It is not because I am particularly attached to concrete, but perhaps it's because I don't particularly like cladding. But I think that attitude is changing. For many of these projects, concrete was the most appropriate solution. And as a material, it is fantastic. The structure and the finished surface are one in the same—there is no need to duplicate.

TG: **What about glass?**

ZH: I like glass.

TG: **How is it working here at BMW? I think its use through the interior of the project can be connected to your earlier investigations in transparent drawings.**

ZH: We had to use glass here. Otherwise the space would become a bunker.

LEFT: Design development rendering
RIGHT: Cladding installation

Cladding installation

TG: **Yes, but you can be very straightforward with glass, or you can push it to do new things. I think you are doing the latter.**

ZH: Well, the budget was very tight here, so we did what we could. I think to use glass within an interior is very different from using it as a cladding or curtain wall.

I have always been interested in transparency. To visit New York, one realizes that transparency is not about making glass facades but rather about the possibility of reflecting five suns at the same time. Our ambitions with glass have to do with making a better environment for the workspace.

TG: **Let's talk more generally about the idea of cladding. The use of the metal and glass skins here brings a very different effect to the project, a direct contrast to the clarity of a concrete wall.**

ZH: In this case, it was different. The structure is still the structure, but in this case, we are enclosed

by five other buildings. Also, it was appropriate to employ industrial materials like metal siding. The siding presented an opportunity to explore new possibilities in cladding.

LT: It is interesting that through all of the initial diagrams, we never investigated the volume of the building. All of the investigations were directed at the occupiable spaces, at the surfaces. There was never a specific investigation of the volume or the building's sculptural quality. This was never the issue.

The design developed into a series of cascading platforms, and of course, we had to enclose this space. Again we turned to the diagrammatic logic of the project, and quickly realized that the solution was to take the planimetric trajectories and wrap them down to form the cladding surfaces.

TG: **Does this project lead you to want to investigate different skins?**

LEFT: Cladding installation
RIGHT: Cladding detail

opposite: Exterior view

ZH: I think it is inevitable. To do a tower, anything above a certain height, one has to consider materials other than concrete. It forces one to engage in transparency and pattern.

TG: **In this building, the patterning on the facades presents the opportunity to map the diagrammatic flows of the project directly on its surfaces.**

ZH: Yes, and you can also see these flows presented as various demarcations on the horizontal surfaces as well.

TG: **So what next?**

ZH: I cannot really say what will be next because I do not know what will come through the door next. We are working on three different master plans at the moment, and we are also working on a few towers. I am interested in pursuing the idea of an urban master plan as an ensemble. That would be my next

ambition—to interpret many buildings together. A city like Singapore is interesting, but in the end, it is still piecemeal. It looks like many cakes on a tray.

TG: **Could we see this ambition as another attempt to get past the twentieth-century obsession with fragmentation and collage?**

ZH: Yes. It is rather a problem of interpreting the relationship between the ground and the interior. In that sense, I am very curious to see the result in Rome. Here we have the beginnings of an ensemble of a large number of pieces, a much higher degree of complexity.

**

London, July 2005

CREDITS

CLIENT
BMW AG, Munich, Germany

DESIGN ARCHITECT
Zaha Hadid Architects, London, UK

ARCHITECTURAL DESIGN
Zaha Hadid with Patrik Schumacher

PROJECT ARCHITECTS
Jim Heverin
Lars Teichmann

DESIGN TEAM
Lars Teichmann
Eva Pfannes
Kenneth Bostock
Stephane Hof
Djordje Stojanovic
Leyre Villoria
Liam Young
Christiane Fashek
Manuela Gatto
Tina Gregoric
Cesare Griffa
Yasha Jacob Grobman
Filippo Innocenti
Zetta Kotsioni
Debora Laub
Sarah Manning
Maurizio Meossi
Robert Sedlak

Niki Neerpasch
Eric Tong

PROJECT TEAM
Matthias Frei
Jan Huebener
Annette Bresinsky
Manuela Gatto
Fabian Hecker
Cornelius Schlotthauer
Wolfgang Sunder
Anneka Wegener
Markus Planteu
Robert Neumayr
Christina Beaumont
Achim Gergen
Caroline Anderson

LANDSCAPE ARCHITECT
Gross. Max, Edinburgh, UK
Bridget Baines
Eelco Hooftman

PROJECT ARCHITECT
Daniel Reiser

STRUCTURAL ENGINEERS
IFB Dr. Braschel AG, Stuttgart, Germany
(Main Structure)
Frank Steller

Anthony Hunts Assoc., London, UK
(Space-Frame Structure)
Les Postawa

MECHANICAL/ELECTRICAL ENGINEERS
IFB Dr. Braschel AG, Stuttgart, Germany
Helmut Kellner

COSTING
AGP Arge Gesamtplanung, Berlin,
Germany
Marcus Hackel
IFB Dr. Braschel AG, Stuttgart, Germany

LIGHTING DESIGN
Equation Lighting, London, UK
Mark Hensman

ACOUSTIC ENGINEER
PMI, Ottobrunn, Germany
Peter Mutard

CIVIL ENGINEER
AGP Arge Gesamtplanung WPW
Ingenieure, Saarbruecken, Germany
Rolf Petzold
Volker Eisenbeis

PROJECT MANAGER
ARGE Projeksteuerung Assmann-
Obermeyer, Munich, Germany
Reiner Reppert

MAIN CONTRACTOR
ARGE Rohbau, Stuttgart, Germany
Herr Pech
Herr Willuhn

STEEL WORKS
Max Bögl Bauunternehmung GmbH &
Co. KG, Neumarkt, Germany
Herr Hierl

FIT-OUT and INTERIOR GLASS
Jaeger Akustik GmbH + Co KG Leipzi
Zwenkau, Germany
Herr Weinrich

FACADE
Radeburger Fensterbau/Schneider
Fertigbau, Stimpfach/Württ., Germany
Herr Bayer

JURY
Architectural jurors
Professor Marc Angélil, Architect,
  Los Angeles/Zurich
Professor Dietrich Fink, Architect, Mu
Guido Hager, Landscape architect, Zu
Christoph Ingenhoven, Architect,
  Düsseldorf
Professor Henning Rambow, Architec
  Leipzig
Professor Matthias Sauerbruch, Archi
  Berlin/London

manent alternate architectural jurors
dine Giseke, Landscape Architect,
erlin
fessor Burkhard Pahl, Architect,
armstadt/Leipzig
e Schumann, Architect, Leipzig

hnical jurors
er Claussen, Senior Vice President
roject Plant Leipzig, BMW AG
nz Cremer, Senior Vice President
echnical Integration, BMW AG
Joachim Fischer, Municipal Councillor
PD Faction, Leipzig
Engelbert Lütke Daldrup, Head
unicipal Building Control, Councillor
rban Development and Construction
ty of Leipzig
Norbert Reithofer, Member of the
oard of Management, BMW AG

manent alternate technical jurors
olaus Bauer, Vice President Logistics
nd IT Project Plant Leipzig, BMW AG
dreas Habicht, Municipal Councillor,
DU fraction, Leipzig
lfgang Kunz, Head Planning
epartment Leipzig
dolf Reichenauer, General Manager
uman Resources Project Plant Leipzig,
MW AG
t Sposta, Vice President Architecture
gineering—Manufacturing, BMW AG

PHOTO CREDITS
All reasonable efforts have been made to
trace the copyright holders of the visual
materials reproduced in this book. The
publisher and the Knowlton School of
Architecture apologize to anyone who
has not been reached. Errors and omissions will be corrected in future editions.

All images courtesy of Zaha Hadid
Architects except as follows:

Courtesy of Bernard Tschumi Architects
17

Photos by Helene Binet
19, 89, 94, 101, 106 top left and top
right, 109, 111 top left, bottom left,
and top right, 112 top left, top right,
and bottom left, 120 top right, 128 left,
129, 143, 147–51, 155, 156

Courtesy of © BMW AG, Photos by Eric
Chmil
111 bottom right, 133, 152

Photos by Roland Halbe
7 top right, 7 center top and center bottom, 93, 100 left, 119 bottom, 120 top
left and bottom, 121, 130–31, 134–35,
136–37, 138, 140, 141, 146, 153,
154, 157

Courtesy of © BMW AG, Photos by
Martin Klindtworth
6 bottom right, 7 top left, 31, 91, 92
right, 96, 98, 99, 104, 105 top left and
top right, 106 bottom, 107, 108 top left
and top right, 112 bottom right, 114 top
right, 115, 126 right, 127, 139, 142,
144–45

Photo by Roger Rothan
14 left

BIOGRAPHY

TODD GANNON is an architect, teacher, and writer
based in Los Angeles. He has taught architectural
theory and design at the Knowlton School of
Architecture, UCLA, and Otis College of Design. In
addition to Source Books in Architecture, his writings
have appeared in *Log*, *Dialogue*, *Loud Paper*, and
elsewhere. He is currently pursuing a doctoral degree
at UCLA.